The Keys to Inner Healing and Deliverance

Lorna Stankoven

CONTENTS

The Keys to Inner Healing and Deliverance

ACKNOWLEDGMENTS

My heart is to give Jesus Christ all the honor and glory in the writing of this book. For this book was truly inspired and written by the Holy Spirit and guided by the heart of God for His children. Without Jesus and His love for me and others, which has been demonstrated through so many healings and miracles, even in my own life, this book would never have been written. Thank you Jesus for all of who You are, for Your faithfulness and love that has been unending towards me through this entire process.

I want to thank my wonderful husband Bill, my sons Devin, Brennan, Garrett and my step-daughter Christina for all their love, support, and for always believing in me, standing with me and loving me unconditionally in all that I am and all that I do. Thank you for sacrificing so much so that I can do the work of the Lord. Words can never express how much you mean to me.

To my church family at Awakening Church, and Women Ministers International, thank you for your love, support, and so many prayers from so many prayer warriors over the years. You mean more to me and the heart of God than you will ever know. You are all pillars of strength, love and encouragement to me and so many others.

I also want to thank Mama Carol, my spiritual mother in the Lord, for without her I would have never had the understanding of Inner Healing or deliverance that I now do. God used you mightily in my life Mama, and to you I will always be so grateful. You are such a true example of a true servant of the Lord with a heart to see the body of Christ risen up in the freedom, power, and authority of Jesus. Thank you for pouring into my life, and into so many in the body of Christ.

1

CHAPTER 1

CAN CHRISTIANS BE OPPRESSED?

What is Inner Healing and Deliverance?

It says in the Bible in Isaiah 61, "He has sent me to bind up and heal the broken hearted, to proclaim liberty to the physical and spiritual captives, and the opening of the prisons and the eyes of those who are bound". That is what the Church is called to do. Inner Healing is the emotional healing of the heart and mind. Deliverance is the release of everything that the enemy has held us captive in through demonic strongholds and oppressions in our lives. As it says in the Bible in Isaiah 61 the Lord wants to make us "oaks of righteousness, lofty, strong and magnificent, distinguished for righteous, justice, and right standing with God, the planting of the Lord". The enemy tries to prevent that from happening in our life by using people, circumstances, and hurts to cause us to be wounded in our hearts and minds. Then we are bound in oppressions or strongholds that prevent us from becoming just that.

What is the Difference Between Possession and Oppression?

Many people get confused and think that Christians cannot be oppressed by the enemy but nothing is farther from the truth. Christians however cannot be possessed. To be possessed infers ownership and the

Devil does not own Christians for we were bought and paid for with a price; the price Jesus paid on the cross.

1 Corinthians 6: 19,20 - NASB

Or do you not know that your body is a temple of the Holy Spirit who is in you, whom you have from God, and that you are not your own? For you have been bought with a price; therefore glorify God in your body.

The definition of possession is "the state of being dominated or controlled by evil spirits, a territory subject to foreign control". It is when someone is owned by someone or something else. We can see the devil cannot possess us because Jesus already does when we are born again.

Oppression is a different story. Oppression means "to be kept down by an unjust use of force or authority, to weigh heavily on, or burdened psychologically, physically, and spiritually". This is what the enemy does to us, even though we are a child of God's. We can be oppressed by the enemy in many ways through the traumas and events in our lives.

Luke 4:18-19 - KJV Jesus reads the Word of God

The Spirit of the Lord is upon me, because he hath anointed me to preach the gospel to the poor; he hath sent me to heal the broken-hearted, to preach

4

deliverance to the captives, and recovering of sight to the blind, to set at liberty them that are bruised.

Luke 4:18-19 - AMP

The Spirit of the Lord is upon Me, because He has anointed Me (the Anointed One, the Messiah) to preach the good news (the Gospel) to the poor, He has sent Me to announce release to the captives and recovery of sight to the blind, to send forth as delivered those who are oppressed (who are downtrodden, bruised, crushed, and broken down by calamity). To proclaim the accepted and acceptable year of the Lord (the day when salvation and the free favors of God profusely abound).

In the Bible Jesus read this in the synagogue and said "today this scripture has been fulfilled in your hearing". Jesus Himself said to set free those who are oppressed, because He understood that although we believe on Him and trust in Him, many of us are oppressed in life.

Psalms 103:6 - NASB

The Lord performs righteous deeds and judgements for all who are oppressed.

The Lord will perform so much for us to set us free from the oppression of the enemy in our lives. As a result not only will we have eternal life but abundant life here on earth. This is what Inner Healing and Deliverance does. It is the power of the Holy Spirit coming into one's life to set them free from every area in which they are oppressed.

We Are Made up of Three Parts

We are made up of three parts: the body, the soul, and the spirit.

The first part is the body, the physical, which is our flesh, blood, muscle, and bones. It is basically every part that makes up our physical being. It is the part that is corruptible, in that it will go back to the dust of the earth when we pass away. It is our earthly body that unfortunately gets old and deteriorates. When we get to heaven we will be given a new body, an incorruptible one. We were never meant to have sickness but because of sin, sickness came into the world and our bodies are now a temporal housing for us until we get to heaven to be with Jesus.

The second part is our soul which is made up of our heart, mind, will and emotions. This part is what makes you, you. It is who you are, your personality, how you tick, how you think, your compassion, all of it. Your will is here too, which is your ability to choose. The will to choose or not to choose is in our soul. The mind is part of our soul and so many wounds are held in the soul, or our mind and heart. The mind holds the conscious and subconscious. The conscious mind is all that you remember, and is where you think and reason each and every day. All of your reasoning and intellectual abilities are in the conscious mind. The mind also holds your subconscious, which is your deep seated thoughts and memories that we do not often remember. It is there where we record all that has ever happened to us. Our subconscious is where the pain of all that has happened in our past is recorded and held even if we have no obvious or recallable memories. This is why the mind and heart hold so many areas of oppression where the enemy keeps us captive. This is where inner healing and deliverance can bring so much freedom to those areas that we are held captive to in our mind and in our heart. Our emotions also reside here in the soul as well. Our emotions are governed by our mind, our heart, and our will. That is why it is said our emotions can lie to us. If we have a lot of pain, wounds, or feel oppressed, our emotions tend to be governed by those areas of pain. This happens in a person in their heart and mind especially in areas of deep rejection and abandonment. That is why we end up acting and reacting out of the places of pain and trauma. During inner healing, the

Holy Spirit is able to go in and heal those places, remove the pain associated with those events, and bring peace and healing. As a result, the emotions associated with the pain and trauma is also released, freeing us from all oppression. We do not forget what happened to us, but now all the pain tied to those events is removed and it no longer holds us captive or oppresses us.

The third area is the spirit. That is the area that communes with God. It is where our conscience is, the area that tells us what is right or wrong. When we get that feeling of "I know I shouldn't do that but I'm going to anyway", that is our conscience. It is also the area, our inner most being, in which the Holy Spirit resides when one becomes born again. It is the place that comes to life in the Spirit when we ask Jesus in our hearts, once again communing with God in a close and personal way that was lost in the Garden of Eden when Adam and Eve fell into sin.

John 7:38 - KJV

He that believes on Me as the scripture hath said, out of his belly shall flow rivers of living water.

We call it our gut. It is in the gut that we get that sense of something that we should or should not do. This is the Holy Spirit speaking to us. It is from there the Holy Spirit flows out to others through our lives. If there are enough areas of oppression in our lives then it makes it harder for the Holy Spirit to flow those rivers of living water through us. Although our lives can be oppressed in our soul, the enemy cannot touch the spirit because it belongs to the Lord, and that is why we cannot be possessed but we can be oppressed. No matter how oppressed we are, the oppression can never rob us of the promise of salvation or eternal life. You belong to Jesus plain and simple. However, the oppression can dramatically affect your quality of life or your ability to function in things of the spirit.

We Need to Remember Who We Are Battling

In all that we are battling within our lives, we need to remember who the oppressor is: the devil. We need to remember that we do not war against flesh and blood.

Ephesians 6:12 - NASB

For our struggle is not against flesh and blood, but against the rulers, against the powers, against the world forces of this darkness, against spiritual forces of wickedness in the heavenly places.

Our real battle is not against other people, our real opposition is the devil.

Greek Translation from "Key Word Study Bible"

Rulers – arche - chief or top in order, place or ranking, top in principality and ruling of darkness. These are the rulers over areas in the demonic realm who are high up in power and ranking.

Powers – exousia- Delegated and given control, influence, authority, jurisdiction, power, right and strength over individuals, situations and events in the demonic realm.

World forces – Kosmokrator - world ruler, is Satan's' forces of darkness, Satan is considered prince of this world, this is referring to Satan and his angels.

Spiritual forces – pneumatikos – demonic entities and spirits of wickedness

Wickedness – poneria – plots of sin, iniquity, depravity, wicked council and deeds, all things evil in nature.

All this is what we battle and the entities with whom we are at war. I did not say this to make us afraid, because we already have victory over it through the cross, but we have been at war with each other for far too long. We have forgotten with whom we are really at war, the devil and his works. For it says in the bible the Devil has come to kill, rob, and destroy. It is him and the works of his darkness that inner healing and deliverance gives us such freedom from. It is his works in our lives through other people and through circumstances that cause us to be oppressed and in bondage.

Through this teaching, the Lord desires to show us every area the enemy and life's circumstances have come to try and put us in bondage. He wants to rob us of all that we could have been for the Kingdom of God. All this was said to give a foundation and to show the need of inner healing and deliverance. It is not only for the lost and those coming into the Kingdom of God, but also for the body of Christ. Jesus came into this world to deliver us from all evil and to destroy the works of the enemy in our lives.

1 John 3:8 - NASB

The one who practices sin is of the devil; for the devil has sinned from the beginning. The Son of God appeared for this purpose, to destroy the works of the devil.

Through inner healing and deliverance, Jesus is able to do just that. It truly is a miracle to watch Him release people from bondages and oppressions that they have struggled with for so many years.

Do Not Do Inner Healing or Deliverance on an Unbeliever

Matthew 12: 43-45 - NASB

Now when the unclean spirit goes out of a man, it passes through waterless places, seeking rest, and does not find it. Then it says, I will return to my house from which I came; and when it comes, it finds it unoccupied, swept, and put in order. Then it goes, and takes along with it seven other spirits more wicked than itself, and they go in and live there; and the last state of that man becomes worse than the first. That is the way it will also be with this evil generation.

I will return in the Bible in the Greek means, "to turn back again upon, or to turn back again against". So if we cast out spirits of the enemy out of a place that is not filled with Jesus and the Holy Spirit, when that spirit tries to enter again it sees that the vessel, or us, is not filled with Jesus and the power of the Holy Spirit. Thus the spirit goes and brings back more than what the person had before, so the person ends up being in worse shape than when they first started. This is really important to note. That is why before entering into ministry we must really make sure the person receiving ministry is aware of this, and have asked the Lord into their hearts. We need to state that this is a journey and a commitment to walking a life out with the Lord, and not just taking advantage of Him to get free. For our freedom always comes through Jesus.

If a person comes to the Lord and then enters into ministry, it is essential that along with ministry, the person sits under the Word in church, as well as having someone in place to disciple them and teach them the Word. The word solidifies the ministry being done, and gives them the foundation on which to stand throughout ministry, as well as when ministry is completed. I have seen in the past that people have been freed by the Lord in a particular area of ministry. The Lord then indicated to me that they had received their healing, but they themselves did not recognize this yet. It was only as they grew stronger in the Word and the teachings of Jesus that they were able to walk out the fullness of their healing. That is why consistently being in church and under the teachings of the Word of God is so important. We need to have the truth of the Word of God to stand on as our foundation to walk out the fullness of our healing in Jesus. Then I watched as they realized they had been made whole and knew in themselves that they were now able to walk into the fullness of their healing with the Lord.

If you are called into this type of ministry you must follow the leading of the Lord, and not the needs of those around you. First of all, if you go upon the need

13

alone you will be overloaded in no time. You will also end up taking upon yourself ministry that is beyond your capabilities, anointing, or knowledge. Also the Lord may say "no" because of the condition of the person. I had one person with whom the Lord told me not to enter into ministry. It was because the person was too weak emotionally and physically and it would have done more harm than good. God told me the person was not able to walk through the healing process. He told me to just leave that person with Him and that through the church services and worship He would perform sovereign ministry within that person that would free them in a way they could handle. God told me I was just to love His child, and that person ended up getting a lot of deliverance and healing from the Lord each week as the Lord moved in their life. Many times that person would come up and tell me how much they had received in the worship and in the church services. Also, the Lord knows the heart of the individual and whether they are serious about doing the work involved in walking through their entire healing. It is important to know whether or not they are dedicated to Jesus and truly want their walk to be a lifestyle, not just a means to a healing. This is really important for them to keep their healing and to walk into the fullness of God for their life. Also some are just simply not ready yet and their hearts are not fully into the process. Only the Lord truly knows all of this. It is also ideal to have the person you are doing ministry with to be in your church or ministry group. It gives you an opportunity to watch over them, and to see how they are reacting and functioning in the Spirit. It also gives you more opportunity to pray for them and to have them receive what they need in a group or church setting.

CHAPTER 2

GIVING THE ENEMY NO PLACE

What we need to understand is how the enemy gains entrance into those places in our lives that causes us to be oppressed. We need to learn how to give the enemy no place or room to occupy in our lives, and how we can be free from the oppression of past pain and traumas.

Ephesians 4:26-27 - KJV

Be ye angry and sin not; let not the sun go down on your wrath; neither give place to the devil.

Ephesians 4:26-27 - AMP

When angry do not sin; do not ever let your wrath, your exasperation, your fury or indignation last until the sun goes down. Leave no such room or foothold for the devil, give no opportunity to him.

The word place, in "neither give place to the devil", means to give him no room or space to occupy in your life. It means to give him no foothold in your life, heart, mind, or body. These footholds or places that the enemy occupies in our lives come from either decisions that we have made that have caused us pain or trauma, or it comes from the places that others have caused us deep pain and wounds in our lives.

Think of a door. You go to try and shut a door so no intruder can get in, but all of a sudden a foot is jammed in the door and you cannot shut it. Now the intruder has access. That is kind of what it is like when the enemy has access through pain, sorrow, and trauma. It can be physical, emotional, or spiritual, but the end result is the same. That foot goes in that door and no matter how hard we try, we can never completely shut that door. That pain gives the enemy a place, a room to occupy. It is as if he sets up a room in your life with which he can move about and cause havoc. It may have come through something someone else did, which is most often the case, but nevertheless the devil now has access. He now has a place in which he can occupy and oppress.

Think of your own home. Your home belongs to you, but the enemy gains access and now sets up house in your study. You still own the house and all the rooms, but there is one room that the enemy managed to get in and set up house through the pain and trauma you keep there. He cannot move from room to room, but has set up a control center in that room or area of pain in your life.

That room becomes a stronghold of the enemy's in our lives. We have not lost our salvation, but the enemy has set up camp so to speak in a wounded area. That room or area the enemy now has control in our mind, our heart, our will and emotions. Each time he pushes that button regarding that wound, rejection or hurt, it triggers all the pain and reactions that go with it. This causes turmoil, pain, and bondage in our lives. God has no authority in that room until we open that door and give Him permission to go in and clean out everything the enemy tried to hide in there, or place in our heart and mind. The longer that place is occupied by the enemy, the larger he would like to make that room. He is never happy with the size of room he has, he always wants more. He desires to expand that place that he now occupies. Whatever pain, rejection, anger, bitterness, or resentment the enemy hides in that room, came in from the original circumstance or trauma and the enemy will continue to use it. He plans to expand that foothold over the years until it makes it hard to even function. The pain or oppression that is hidden in that room will eventually pop up in our life from time to time as circumstances trigger those memories of pain. The devil's desire is to build all these small places he occupies into fortresses from which he can occupy to wreak havoc in your life and on the lives of others around you. He wants to use it to discredit you and to completely discredit God.

Acts 5: 1-5 - AMP

But a certain man named Ananias, with his wife Sapphira, sold a piece of property, and kept back (hid) some of the price for himself, with his wife's full knowledge, and bringing a portion of it he laid it at the apostles feet. But Peter said Ananias, why has Satan filled your heart to lie to the Holy Spirit, and to keep back some of the price of the land? While it remained unsold, did it not remain your own? And after it was sold, was it not under your control? Why is it that you have conceived this deed in your heart? You have not lied to men, but to God. And as he heard these words Ananias fell down and breathed his last; and great fear came upon all who heard of it.

It was not only Ananias that died but also his wife as she lied as well. There was a stronghold of greed and fear that grew in the hearts of these two. Notice it says Satan filled their heart. He is the one who put those lies in their heart to begin with, which they believed that gave him a place or space to occupy. It started with fear of not having enough, then it progressed into greed, and finally the lies the enemy spoke to them caused fortresses to be built in their hearts for the enemy to dwell. All this caused them to go before Peter and lie to him and the Holy Spirit. They were never told to give it all. That was their choice, and that was what Peter was telling them. Ananias and Sapphira did not have to give anything, but their lying to the Holy Spirit cost them their lives. God wanted that first move of the Church to remain pure.

God wants a militant church, which means a church not afraid of going to war with the enemy, but also a church that is not afraid of going after the strongholds in their own lives. The strongholds, or fortresses in our lives, prevent the true move of God moving through us to accomplish God's heart. Many times, we do not even realize the strongholds that are within us, because we have lived with them for so long that it just seems normal. However, the power and anointing of the Holy Spirit is able to expose those oppressions and strongholds to get rid of them through inner healing and deliverance. Remember you have authority over every stronghold in your life through the name of Jesus. He told us in the

Bible, "not only these things shall you do but you shall do greater things".

God desires a Church and a people that are free and able to move with His Spirit to accomplish His purposes on this earth. He desires to open every door to every room that the enemy occupies, so we can truly be free from oppression. For He told us in His Word, "when you are free, you are free indeed". We then become a testimony of the love, kindness and power of a Savior that died and provided us with true freedom in every area of our life.

CHAPTER 3

BINDING AND LOOSING

Jesus has already accomplished everything that we will ever need on the cross. He has bound and loosed in the spirit everything that will ever come against us. He accomplished it in the same way that He took every sin onto Himself, so we could be forgiven and have eternal life.

Matthew 16: 15-19 - NASB

He said to them, "But who say you that I am?" And Simon Peter answered and said, "Thou art the Christ, the Son of the Living God." And Jesus answered and said to him, "Blessed are you Simon Barjona because flesh and blood did not revealed this to you, but my Father who is in heaven. And I also say to you that you are Peter, and upon this rock I will build My church and the gates of Hades shall not overpower it. I will give you the keys of the kingdom of heaven; and whatever you shall bind on earth shall be bound in heaven; and whatsoever you shall loose on earth shall be loosed in heaven.

Greek Translation of Key Word Study Bible

To bind – to chain, to bind together, bind around, fasten, to put in bonds, to knit, to tie, to forbid

To loose – to break, to dissolve, to put off, to unbind, to untie, to loosen that which is bound, to set free, to make void, to do away with, dissolve, release, deliver

Notice in this passage Jesus says He is giving us the keys to the Kingdom of Heaven. It is those keys that bind and loose the things that the enemy tries to use against us, and oppress us with. Jesus won the keys of death and the grave when He died on the cross. He won everything back that the enemy stole in the fall of man. Jesus has already bound everything that can come against us and we already have victory over it all. We just need to know how to apply it in our lives. Whatever we pray for and bind in the physical world, it is immediately bound in the spiritual, and whatever you bind in the spiritual is immediately bound in the physical. We have the authority to tie up, to chain, to forbid any spirits moving through a person, or around them, to come against us, or manipulate us in any way. Any spirit that has come against us, and put us into bondage can be bound up, tied up, fastened, put into bonds, and then loosed off of us or someone else by praying it to be loosed off. To loose means that through the authority in the name of Jesus we can command it to set us free, untie, dissolve, and break that which has tied us or bound us up. We are then set free from that which bound us and made it hard for us to go forward in certain areas in our lives.

This is a major key to walking a walk with Jesus that is free from every burden and oppression that the enemy would want to put on us. It is surprising how many do not even know about this or feel that it is no longer relevant and no longer needed. It has been an essential key in doing inner healing and deliverance and seeing the captives set free. Jesus said in the Bible He was giving us the "keys to the Kingdom of heaven", the keys that unlock the things of the spirit. Binding and loosing are one of those keys. He showed me once as I received a set of keys, a long hall with many cupboards along the sides. He told me that the keys we receive as we walk on our life's journey, would unlock each of these doors to each of these cupboards. In each cupboard would be more things that we would be able to use in our walk with the Lord. The keys He would give would unlock many mysteries and understanding to what the cross provided for each one of us, and how to use it for the glory of God and His Kingdom. Binding and loosing is one of those keys.

Luke 13:11-16 - KJV

And behold, there was a woman which had a spirit of infirmity eighteen years, and was bowed together, and could in no wise lift up herself. And when Jesus saw her, he called her to him, and said unto her, woman thou art loosed from thine infirmity. And He laid His hands on her and immediately she was made straight, and glorified God. And the ruler of the synagogue answered with indignation, because Jesus had healed on the Sabbath day, and said unto the people, there are six days in which men ought to work; in them therefore come and be healed, and not on the Sabbath day. The Lord then answered him, and said, thou hypocrite, doth not each one of you on the Sabbath loose his ox or his ass from the stall, and lead him away to watering? And ought not this woman, being a daughter of Abraham, whom Satan hath bound, lo these eighteen years be loosed from this bond on the Sabbath day?

This woman was bound with a spirit of infirmity for eighteen years and you can bet they would have tried all conventional means to heal her, but nothing worked. She remained riddled in pain on the floor. Jesus tells us it was a spirit of infirmity that put the woman in that state. However, with the authority we have in Jesus, we can do the same thing that Jesus did. When Jesus loosed the woman, He had really first bound (to tie, chain, forbid) that spirit of infirmity by not permitting it to move against the woman any longer. He then loosed it, or released it from the woman therefore setting her free. We have the authority to do the same in His name. We can bind and loose all things such as, depression, anxiety, fear, and so much more. Listen to whatever the Holy Spirit tells you through the word of knowledge, and then loose if off the person, or yourself. This means to have the spirit untied from the person, or set free, dissolved, released and delivered from whatever was binding them.

Acts 2:24 - KJV

Whom God hath raised up having loosed the pains of death because it was not possible that he should be holden of it.

Isaiah 58:6 - KJV

Is not this the fast that I have chosen? To loose the bands of wickedness, to undo the heavy burdens and to let the oppressed go free, and that ye break every yoke?

These two verses show what the Lord has taken authority over. We too now have authority through Jesus to loose the bands of wickedness and the burdens that we or others carry, so we can live free in Jesus. Jesus has loosed or delivered us from the pains of death. We have eternal life because when He died on the cross, Jesus loosed the chains of death from around us and gave us life.

Psalm 116:6 - KJV

O Lord truly I am thy servant, and the son of thine handmaid; thou hast loosed my binds.

Psalm 107: 9, 10 - KJV

For he satisfieth the long soul, and filleth the hungry soul with goodness. Such as sit in darkness and in the shadow of death being bound in affliction and iron.

This shows how even in the Old Testament that the Psalmists understood that it was only the Lord who can loose the binds of iron with which this life tries to trap us. It is by His authority alone that He achieved through His sacrifice on the cross that we are able to do this.

Revelation 9:14-15 - KJV

Saying to the sixth angel which had the trumpet, Loose the four angels which are bound in the great river Euphrates. And the four angels were loosed, which were prepared for an hour, and a day, and a month, and a year, for to slay the third part of men.

This shows how God even binds, or ties, or fastens, or holds even the angels from doing their assignment until the time is at hand. At the right moment, they will be set free or loosed to carry out judgment on mankind who rejected God. The Lord has the ability to hold back anything on this earth, whether it be his angels from doing certain tasks or the enemy from carrying out his tactics. All of it is under His jurisdiction because of what He accomplished on the cross.

Revelation 20: 2-3 - KJV

And He laid hold on the dragon, that old serpent, which is the Devil and Satan, and bound him a thousand years, and cast him into the bottomless pit, and shut him up, and set a seal upon him, that he should deceive the nations no more, till the thousand years should be fulfilled and after that he must be loosed a little season.

This verse shows the ultimate power and authority of God and His ability to bind and loose. He will be able to bind Satan and keep him bound one thousand years until he is let loose to deceive man one final time. People will walk by and look at him and he will be bound helpless, thinking this is the guy that brought so much havoc on earth. This is the power of the Lord and His ability to bind Satan and his works.

Binding and loosing is truly an incredible tool to have in your spiritual tool box. It is a key that allows you to have great victory over all that will come against you to try and rob, dishearten, and bind you in any way. Jesus already finished the work on the cross, we just need to learn how to use all the authority that he claimed back for His Church and each believer.

How Binding and Loosing and The Gifts of The Spirit Are Used

Binding, loosing and the gifts of the spirit are essential when doing inner healing and deliverance. All will be functioning when administering inner healing and deliverance whether to yourself or others. Binding and loosing are not used enough in prayer before hand, whether in a church setting or in individual ministry before proceeding into the service or prayer. It is essential to bind up all manifestations of the demonic in people in both applications. The enemy would love to manifest and display who he is to take away and distract from what God is doing. Whether in church or in ministry, we need to completely bind up the enemy and forbid him to move, operate, or act out in any fashion so that the Lord can have His way in our churches and in our ministry sessions. This is essential for the Lord to move unhindered and for the person you are ministering to or yourself, to have a session that is ordered by God without hindrance.

Let us look at the Church setting for one minute. We need to bind according to Ephesians 6:12, and forbid every spirit to speak out, or act out in any way shape or form. It is critical to give the Lord full authority, rule, dominion and Lordship in the church in Jesus name. When we do this before our church services or even prayer sessions we have bound up, forbidden, and tied up the enemy from moving in the service and causing distractions of any kind. Distractions individually or corporately make it hard for individuals to hear the message and receive the Word of God. We need to give the Lord the authority and ability to move and remove anything at any time that He desires to do. We want the Lord to have His way in our services and in our prayer sessions so He can accomplish His heart and His plans. We do not want the enemy to disrupt this, or for any individual to be robbed. If we got into the practice of having intercession before church and meetings, binding the work of the enemy, we would start to see a greater move of God where His hand is free to move uninhibited. It is also a way to truly align our hearts with God's.

It is also a great tool to use individually in our daily lives. So many times we deal with people who have issues of anger, control, manipulation, and other such things, that when we bind up that which operates through them we find we end up having so much less turmoil in our own lives. That is why as was mentioned before, we need to remember who we are battling, principalities and powers, not people. So use this in key situations in your daily life, situations at work, or with family. Have you ever come home and your spouse has had a bad day and is grumpy because of dealing with some tough situations at work and you end up getting the brunt of it? Bind all tiredness, fatigue, anger, and resentment in them and forbid it to be directed to you. It will be amazing how the person just seems to settle down. It is really all that they went through that day acting out against you. It really works! The one thing that needs to be noted is that you cannot bind up the flesh. You can only bind up spirits from functioning through people. If you bind up a particular spirit and nothing happens, there is a good chance it is because it is the flesh acting out and not a spirit. We need to kill off the flesh in our own lives, it cannot be bound.

One day I was parking in the parking lot outside a pharmacy, and what happened next truly showed me the power of binding and loosing. As I got out of the car, a man at the exact same time jumped out of a van next to me. He proceeded to open the door for me as I walked inside. I felt incredibly uncomfortable and uneasy. As I walked up the isle of the pharmacy I noticed that he was following me. As I quickly went to the next isle, he appeared at the other end of the same isle. Saying it was creepy is an understatement. I began to bind up lust, but it made no difference. I went to the next isle, and once again he appeared at the other end of the same isle. I immediately went to God and asked Him what it was. God told me to bind a spirit of stalking and to command it to leave the store in Jesus name. I did just that and as I went to the next isle I realized that he was no longer there. As I walked to the front of the pharmacy, I looked out the window to where my car and his van had been parked when I noticed that not only had he left the pharmacy, but the van was also gone. God explained to me that He allowed this incident to show me the power of binding and loosing in something that I could actually see. I have never forgotten it to this day. This truly elevated my faith in how powerful this tool is for the Church and us as individuals to walk in the power and authority of Jesus.

Binding and loosing is essential when starting any ministry session in inner healing and deliverance. In every session I bind every spirit according to Ephesians 6:12, and I bind and forbid them to act out in any way shape or form. The only way they will move is when the Lord is releasing them from someone's life in Jesus name. I also seal the room in the blood and in the power of the Holy Spirit giving the Lord full dominion, authority, and Lordship over the session. I ask the Lord to release His anointing onto each person in the room, and to release His gifts of the Spirit to each person, and for them to operate in the fullness of what they are in Jesus name. This is essential for each session, especially for people that have been through a lot and have had much trauma in their lives, or have been in any form of witchcraft practices. It gives the Lord full authority over the session with His gifts flowing in full operation. You will notice His presence entering the room and it will give you and the person you are ministering to a real sense of peace. Give the Lord full Lordship over your prayers for yourself, or in a session for another. Ask the Lord to give you or the person you are praying for the eyes to see, the ears to hear and the heart to understand what the Spirit is saying. This will really help you receive all that the Lord wants to give you. You should always have more than just yourself in the prayer room when doing ministry for someone else, especially in the beginning. Jesus after all sent out the disciples two by two to minister to the people. Another advantage to having someone with you is the other person acts as a witness on your behalf to the content of the session. Furthermore, the person is another ear to hear the Lord, so you can work as a team for the person to whom you are ministering to. I have consent forms that I get most people to sign that come from outside of our church. This gives written consent and release in doing this type of prayer ministry. It is purely a protective measure that unfortunately is an important thing to have in place in the times we live in.

All the gifts of the Spirit are in full operation in sessions of inner healing and deliverance. That is why it is so important to learn in our Christian walks how to hear God. It is something that we tend to overlook, and not train our hearts to hear that still small voice. Inner healing is always led by the Holy Spirit, not by us. I cannot state this strongly enough. We never direct the session for ourselves or others, as that is the job of the Holy Spirit. He is in full control and will direct where and how the session is to go, not us, even if God reveals to us where the pain is located. We need to let the Holy Spirit lead the entire session. That is why the gifts of the spirit must be in full operation. The gifts of word of knowledge and word of wisdom, are so important to following the leading of the Holy Spirit in what is to be done and in what order. There is also healing of the heart and of the mind- through the gift of healing- that will work throughout the session. The discerning of spirits tells us what demonic strongholds are there, and what emotional wounds the person is carrying. All deliverance is always the working of the gift of miracles. Every deliverance is a miracle of God. God will even use prophecy in the session to give His heart to the individual, and to bring deep healing into their hearts and lives. It truly is an amazing move of God to see Him go in and bring healing and relief to the deepest areas of pain in someone's life. It is something you never get tired of seeing. We will get into more depth of how each of these gifts are used in inner healing and deliverance later on. However, the gifts of the spirit and binding and loosing are all essential to moving in the ministry of inner healing and deliverance.

You will find that the Lord will use His believers for simple inner healing and deliverance, and will flow the gifts of the spirit through them as needed. He will use it to bring healing when going as an individual before Him in prayer. You will be surprised how the Lord will move for you, to bring healing in your heart, mind, body, and soul. He truly just waits for us to come to Him to ask for what we need.

Mark 16: 17,18 - NASB

These signs will accompany those who have believed; in My name they will cast out demons, they will speak with new tongues. They will pick up serpents and if they drink any deadly poison it will not hurt them. They will lay hands on the sick and they will recover.

Notice it says that these signs shall follow those who believe. The Lord will truly use His Church to set the captives free and to heal the broken hearted. The Lord is the same yesterday, today, and forever, using His Church to save and heal those that so desperately need Him.

However, for more complicated cases, where the pain and trauma are deep and severe, or where there are witchcraft or occult practices, it will require someone who is more experienced in moving in the gifts of the spirit to lead them through the healing process. Anyone that has had sexual, emotional or physical abuse would fit into this category as well. The wounds and trauma will be deeper and require more ministry over a longer period of time. However, know that when you go before God and ask Him for healing in areas in your life, He will always meet you, and move on your behalf.

When dealing in witchcraft or occult practices if you are praying for another person, never open someone up in that area without having a person who has had some experience in that with you. It would be key to have them functioning as a mentor and consultant when doing ministry on yourself or on others. This is why it is so important to follow the leading of the Holy Spirit. Let Him lead you as to where you are to go in prayer for yourself, and in what order, or if you are to go into prayer at all for another person. Remember He knows all about you and those you may minister to. He will always lead you in the perfect order and in the perfect way.

CHAPTER 4

FORGIVENESS

Unforgiveness, bitterness, and resentment are some of the most common reasons that the enemy has access to many people's lives. The devil has a legal right to occupy our hearts and minds when unforgiveness is present. The devil is very legalistic and looks for loopholes and openings to put that foot in the door, so he can occupy that room we talked about earlier. Unforgiveness is a huge reason the enemy is occupying rooms in Christian's hearts and minds.

Many think they have forgiven others, but they have given mental forgiveness but not forgiveness of the heart. They know it is something they need to do, and are called to do, but it has not been done with the heart, only the mind. Mind forgiveness does not shut those doors, or toss the enemy out of those rooms that he is occupying. It must be deep forgiveness of the heart to truly release all unforgiveness, bitterness, and resentment. Anything short of that leaves the person still in bondage.

Matthew 18: 32-35 AMP

Then his master called him and said to him, You contemptible and wicked attendant. I forgave and cancelled all that great debt of yours because you begged me to. And should you not have had pity and mercy on your fellow attendant, as I had pity and mercy on you? And in wrath his master turned him over to the torturers (tormentor, jailers), till he should pay all that he owed. So also My heavenly Father will deal with every one of you if you do not freely forgive your brother from your heart his offenses.

Notice we will be turned over to the tormentor or torturer, because unforgiveness is of the devil and brings torment. We end up being bound to those we do not forgive. Think of a ball and chain. It is as if we are tied with a ball and chain to those we do not forgive. It is like you can never forget that person. They are always on your mind, always nagging at you, pushing your buttons even when they may not even be in your life any longer. Every time their name comes up it irritates you. That ball and chain is always a weight around your feet and an opening that has given the enemy a place or room to occupy in your life.

Over and over again in ministry, I find that very few people forgive from the heart when coming to a place of forgiveness. In inner healing and deliverance you will find that when you are praying for yourself or others, you will try to ask the Lord to release something in your life and for some reason it just will not release off of your heart or mind. Many times it is because unforgiveness is still there. The Lord will often tell you, if you listen, that the person, or yourself, needs to release forgiveness to someone in that situation in order to get their healing.

In some cases, when there are things such as abuse or rape involved, it is so much harder for a person to release forgiveness, which is totally understandable. You sometimes will have to ask the Lord to show you, or the person you are praying for, the heart of the person, or what happened in their lives that caused them to hurt someone like that. The Lord showed me many years ago, that hurting people hurt people. The wounds and pain in their own lives, and boundaries crossed, or boundaries never even established, caused them to do horrible things to others. I have seen this over and over again. The Lord goes in and will show us the motives behind why they did what they did, and what caused them to take such actions. The Lord, in His mercy and love, through the gifts of the Spirit will often show you, or another, the pain of the person, and why they did it. He then gives us or the person we are ministering to the supernatural ability to forgive from the heart, the person who hurt them so deeply. It is amazing to watch. Sometimes if you or another person is having a hard time, you can get them to write a letter, addressing it to the person, explaining all they did to them that caused them so much pain. Many times after writing the letter and getting all the pain written down they are able to forgive that person. The letter does not need to be sent, as it is one way for the person to release their emotions. Forgiveness does not mean what they did was okay; it is releasing them to Jesus and forgiving them as Jesus forgave us.

Ephesians 4:31,32 - AMP

Let all bitterness and indignation and wrath (passion, rage, bad temper) and resentment (anger, animosity) and quarreling (brawling, clamor, contention) and slander (evil-speaking, abusive or blasphemous language) be banished from you, with all malice (spite, ill will, or baseness of any kind). And become useful and helpful and kind to one another, tender-hearted (compassionate, understanding, loving-hearted), forgiving one another (readily and freely) as God in Christ forgave you.

Matthew 18: 21,22 - NASB

Then Peter came and said to Him, Lord, how often shall my brother sin against me and I forgive him? Up to seven times? Jesus said to him, I do not say to you, up to seven times, but to seventy times seven.

From these two scriptures, you can see that we are truly called to forgive one another indefinitely, without measure or end. It is hard to do when you have been wronged and hurt so deeply, but we need to understand that forgiveness is about us. Forgiveness sets us free to go on and live a full life. However, it does not let the other person off the hook. When you forgive even from deep wounds, you hand that person over to the Lord, for as it says in the Bible He is judge, jury, and vengeance is His. When we have not forgiven them, it is like we are bound to them wanting to bring punishment and judgment on them ourselves for what they did to us. When we forgive we are free, and have handed them over to the Lord. I have seen time and time again that the way He brought correction into someone's life for what they did to me, was way better than what I would have ever come up with on my own. So in the end, do we want to deal with our trespassers, or do we want the Lord to handle them? I want Him to, for He is just, His ways are higher, and His wisdom is greater. In the end, I really want the person to see the error of their ways so that they do not hurt anyone else. Forgiveness releases us to move on with our lives. It is not as if the circumstance never happened, but when we forgive, we are no longer bound to the pain that person brought. We have the memory, but all the pain associated with it is gone.

Another area we struggle with in forgiveness is forgiving ourselves. We carry the grace and mercy when it comes to others, but when it comes to ourselves that is a different matter. We hold ourselves to such a high standard that sometimes we cannot release forgiveness to ourselves. This is really typical in people that are perfectionists. This hinders us as much as not forgiving another person. In fact, it can make things even harder, because we see ourselves as failures, or as not being good enough. As a result, we then take on shame and guilt. In those places we usually let in self-condemnation, self-loathing, and self-hatred. These can be spiritual or emotional, but either way it needs to be released along with unforgiveness, bitterness, resentment, shame, and guilt. If you are carrying any of these emotions towards yourself ask the Lord if you have any unforgiveness and where it first entered into your life, so you can forgive yourself. He will then release all these emotions that have been tormenting you for so long.

As you notice by the scripture in Ephesians, there are certain spirits that work together in unforgiveness. Most times when you are in prayer, and the person has forgiven those who have hurt them, you will then ask the Lord to release unforgiveness, bitterness, and resentment from them. These three always tend to come together and work together. They can just be emotional, but if the unforgiveness has been there a while there are most likely spirits of unforgiveness, bitterness, and resentment that need to be released. As stated earlier on, these spirits do not possess a person but they are functioning in a room that the enemy is occupying in a person's life and heart. So we give the Lord permission to go into that room, or stronghold, by forgiving that person and thus evicting the tenants of unforgiveness, bitterness, and resentment. Also, release anything else the Lord will give you to release. The person will immediately feel the release of all that they were carrying. It will feel to them that they are lighter and carrying so much less. It is amazing how it makes such an immediate impact and difference.

If unforgiveness , bitterness, and resentment have been there a long time, this may mean that there may be other spirits that may have to be released. When dealing with anger, rage and wrath, which can come in through deep seated unforgiveness, you must release the angels to come hold the person. The angels are ministers to the heirs of salvation and when in ministry, they can help more than you know. If a demon of anger is present, it is one that can come out with extreme force and strength. When you ask the angels to come hold, they will literally hold the person in the chair so neither you or the person you are ministering to would become injured from that spirit as it releases. Many times I have seen the angels literally sit a person down or hold a person's arms to their sides so that I or the person I am doing ministry with does not get hurt. The person remains calm as the Lord releases all anger, and rage. Anger is a spirit that is toxic, eating a person up inside, making it impossible to move forward. When doing ministry in forgiveness, always know that there may be other emotions or spirits that need to be released. Always let the Holy Spirit speak to you as to what He wants to release from the person. This is why inner healing and deliverance is always guided and directed by the Holy Spirit.

Example of How To Pray To Forgive Someone

First of all remember to bind everything according to Ephesians 6:12. Then release God's anointing and the gifts of the Spirit. Then give Jesus Lordship over your prayer time and ask Him to give you the eyes to see the ears to hear and the heart to understand what the Holy Spirit is about to speak or show you.

Now ask the Lord to show you if there is anyone that you have unforgiveness towards. As was mentioned before He may show you someone that you thought you had forgiven. If Jesus brings a name to your mind it is because you gave mental forgiveness but not heart forgiveness. Proceed to ask the Lord why the person did what they did and what caused them to hurt you in that way. Give Him a chance to speak to your heart and show you. It will bring great understanding. Many times it will be because they themselves were hurt so badly in the same manner. Really listen and feel with your heart what they went through because it is from there you will forgive them. When I went into my own life with the Lord years ago, He showed me I had unforgiveness to two people who had raped me. I thought well how do I forgive that. He showed me why they did it. Although I saw two large overpowering men, God showed me that they saw themselves as so small and insignificant, without strength or control in their lives. He showed me that they hated themselves and felt weak. Jesus then spoke to me and told me that when they did what they did it made them feel strong in that moment, and how sad it really was that they had to do that to a woman to feel strong. Jesus showed me how they were tormented by this and that I could be free, but they would still be living in this torment of feelings of weakness and unworthiness. In that moment due to the understanding Jesus gave me about them, I was immediately able to forgive them and release them to Jesus. To this day, I give my testimony easily about the healing that I received when the Lord released all the pain and healed all my wounds of unforgiveness in this area. All that is left now is just a memory that testifies to the greatness of our Lord.

CHAPTER 5

DEALING WITH ROOT ISSUES

Going to the roots of issues in inner healing and deliverance is key when doing ministry. The root issue is the first time that this belief system, wound or trauma first came into one's life. We must minister from this root to allow full healing in any area whether emotional or spiritual. To not do so is to leave wounded areas, pain, and insecurities not fully dealt with. This enables these areas to once again grow and fester in one's life.

Why It Is Important To Go To The Roots Of An Issue

Matthew 15:13 - AMP

He answered, Every plant which My heavenly Father has not planted will be torn up by the roots

You see every plant that the enemy has planted will grow into thorns and thistles choking out the Lord and the truth of God. It will continue to grow hindering our lives in many ways. These plants are really our insecurities, feelings of unworthiness, fears, angers, and resentments. All must be pulled out at the roots for them to never grow again in someone's life.

Think of a weed in your garden, or on your sidewalk. When you just pull out the part that is showing above the ground, it looks like it is gone, but the root system is still in place. Then what happens in about two weeks is that the weed is back, and it seems even bigger than what it was when you first pulled it out. That is how it works in the spiritual. When we just pull out the things we need to deal with at the surface level that insecurity or bitterness just grows back again because the root system is still in place. The root system in a plant is its source of life. It gives the plant its water and nutrients. It is the same in the spiritual. The root that the enemy planted through trauma and pain gives new life to that bitterness, anger, or insecurity again. Before you know it, you are back to where you started. This is why it is imperative to go back to the root of an issue, where that feeling of insecurity (or whatever you are dealing with) first came into your life. Without doing this, you will never fully be free.

Hebrews 12:14,15 - AMP

Strive to live in peace with everybody and pursue that consecration and holiness without which no one will (ever) see the Lord. Exercise foresight and be on the watch to look (after one another) to see that no one falls back from and fails to secure God's grace (His unmerited favor and spiritual blessing) in order that no root of resentment (rancor, bitterness, or hatred) shoots forth and causes trouble and bitter torment and the many become contaminated and defiled by it.

What we do not realize is that when we allow these roots of issues and pain to remain in us, they not only hurt and defile us, but those around us. They end up coming out on all those whom we care about. That is why we need to weed out all the pain, wounds and issues in our lives that the enemy has planted. They need to be pulled out by the roots. Notice that it says new shoots can come forth from those roots that cause torment. The enemy has put those roots into our lives to cause just that, torment. For as long as we are dealing with all the torment that these roots cause in our lives, we will never walk into the fullness of God. We will always end up in a cycle of torment.

God gave me the analogy one time of a tube of toothpaste. If you want to get all the toothpaste out of the tube, it is much better to start squeezing the toothpaste tube from the bottom, rolling it up. When we try and squeeze it out from about halfway up or higher, it really makes it harder to get all the rest of the toothpaste out that remains at the bottom of the tube.   We all desire to weed out of our lives all that the enemy has planted. The best place to start is at the root or the first place that particular lie or wound came in. When you let God minister to you from the root of that particular issue, then it is so much easier to remove all the sequential types of lies or wounds that came in after the root cause.

How To Minister To The Roots Of Pain That Surfaces

Matthew 3:10 - NASB

And the axe is already laid at the root of the trees; every tree therefore that does not bear good fruit is cut down and thrown into the fire.

Many oppressions act as root systems in our lives that the

Lord goes in and removes, but the Lord is saying His ax is lying at the root of the trees that will not bear fruit. He is waiting to cut down and remove everything in our lives that the enemy has grown, which will not bear good fruit. With His ax He will cut down the very root system that established all the torment and pain.

That is why when doing inner healing and deliverance it is so important to ask the Lord to take yourself or the person you are praying for to the root of what they are struggling with. If a person has a fear of something, or insecurity in an area, ask the Lord to take that person to the root of that insecurity or fear in Jesus name. The Holy Spirit will bring back to the person's mind the root or the first time that fear entered into their life. As previously stated, pulling out by the roots the fear or insecurity where it first entered in makes it so much easier to release all similar oppressions that came in after that point.

As I explained before, you always let the Holy Spirit lead in all ministry. He is the one who directs and leads. He knows where the roots are that even you may have forgotten, or have just not considered even important. Nevertheless, those incidents that the Lord takes you to are so important in removing the roots of where that first deception or pain came. That is why it is so important to not lead the session yourself but to let the Holy Spirit have full control.

To pray for an individual or yourself, first you bind according to Ephesians 6:12. Release all the gifts of the

Holy Spirit, and ask the Lord to release His anointing to give you the eyes to see, the ears to hear, and the heart to understand. Ask the Lord to bring up from your mind and heart the root of the fear, or pain that you or a person is dealing with. You will find the Lord may take you or a person back to when they were very young, when that fear was first established in their lives. Ask Jesus to appear to you or the person you are ministering to in that place so they feel safe with Him as the memory comes up. After they receive the memory, ask the Lord to bring up all the pain and trauma related to that event. Then pray for the Lord to release from them the fear and anything else that the Lord gives you through the word of knowledge that came in through the trauma. Then ask the Lord to speak the truth about that particular situation into your or their life. It is always more powerful if you or the individual can hear the truth for yourself from the Lord. If you are praying for an individual and they are still having a hard time hearing what the Lord is saying to them, then share what the Lord is giving you about their situation. Take the time to make sure they understand the truth and revelation about their situation as it will have powerful results in their lives going forward. Always take the time to make sure you get everything released emotionally or spiritually in that memory. To hurry over memories because we think that they are not important enough, is to not give yourself or an individual the fullness of healing that the Lord desires. Remember, not everything is spiritual; some of what you are releasing is emotional but has caused just as much heartache in your or their life as anything spiritual.

When you are ministering, always look at the person you are ministering to, and check to see if they are struggling physically in any way when you are releasing a particular spirit or emotion. If you can see them struggling a bit, then it means you need to spend more time on that particular emotion or spirit to make sure it is all gone and nothing is left. This would also apply to when you are praying for yourself. Take the time to release it all to the Lord. It is so important as I stated before to not rush through, to make sure you or the person you are ministering to is able to have the time you or they need to release everything to Jesus.

You will be using this in inner healing and deliverance with much frequency as things come up in your life, or in a person's life that you are ministering to. If you are doing ministry on yourself, it is always advisable to have someone with you that you trust who can pray for you as you are going through the process. That person may also get information for you through the Lord that you are to receive. Remember to always start with the root cause. The root anchors all the other deception and pain that reinforces that first lie about their life. With the anchor removed, there is no longer that initial trauma for similar pain to latch onto in the future. The Lord is waiting to uproot everything the enemy has planted. This is such a major key in all inner healing and deliverance.

CHAPTER 6

GENERATIONAL CURSES

This area of ministry has become quite controversial in the past years. The reason is that it is misunderstood, but is such an important key in inner healing and deliverance. If a Christian can become oppressed by the enemy in areas of pain and fears, then a Christian can most certainly end up with generational strongholds that have been passed down from the parents to the child. Most people have not been Christians all their lives so the enemy has had lots of time to legally pass through the generations the oppressions or strongholds of the parents. This is why when you look back at your own life, or at others, you will see many of the same struggles in the parents and in the children.

Exodus 20: 5,6 - AMP

You shall not make yourself any graven image (to worship) or any likeness of anything that is in the heavens above, or that is in the earth beneath, or that is in the water under the earth. You shall not bow down yourself to them or serve them; for I the Lord your God am a jealous God, visiting the iniquity of the fathers upon the children to the third and fourth generation of those who hate Me.

Exodus 34:6,7 - NASB

Then the Lord passed by in front of him, and proclaimed The Lord! The Lord God compassionate and gracious, slow to anger, and abounding in lovingkindness and truth. Who keeps mercy and loving kindness for thousands, forgives iniquity and transgression and sin, yet He will by no means leave the guilty, unpunished visiting the iniquity of the fathers upon the children and the grandchildren to the third and fourth generation. (Deuteronomy 5: 9,10)

Clearing Up Misconceptions of Generational Curses

In the natural, physical and emotional traits pass from generation to generation. Some are good traits like a sense of humor and others are bad, like a bad temper or being impatient, for example. As there is a natural umbilical cord that flows nutrients and all that the baby needs to the womb. There is one that acts like a spiritual umbilical cord that flows the spiritual component of the parents to the children. Now it says in the word that we do not pay for the sins of the parents, and that is completely true. This is where the misunderstanding comes in. When we come to the Lord, we are saved and the ransom is paid in full. We are bought and paid for with a price, and we belong to Jesus. Thus we will not see spiritual death, nor pay the price for our own sins, or the sins of our father or mother. Jesus has already taken care of that. However, generational oppression is much different than paying the price for sin. Because of our natural blood lines in families, the oppressions of the father and the mother are able to pass through the generations to us legally. Now those spiritual oppressions that operated in the mother and father are now trying to take the same hold in our life. Even as Christians the oppressions of the parents can try and take root. We however have the authority through the name of Jesus to cut those oppressions off in the generations. If we, or someone we are ministering to, does not know the Lord, then those generational curses are able to go from one generation to another without much opposition.

We also need to understand how important it is to learn to appropriate the cross in our life. Even though we are now His, we need to take the power and authority that we now have through the cross and use it in our lives. We need to release ourselves in prayer from the strongholds that have hampered our parent's lives in the generations. We no longer have to battle the same oppressions. As soon as we ask Jesus in our hearts, all that is oppressing us generationally has no right to be there, but through either sin or not understanding what our inheritance and authority is in Jesus, we do not see that we now have the authority to tell it to leave in Jesus name. We now have the legal right to tell all oppressions that functioned in the generations to leave, because we now belong to Jesus. Remember, the devil does not play by the rules, and has always tried to take what is not his, or rob us of what belongs to us. It is like a squatter that is in a vacant building. He does not have a right to be there because someone else owns the building, but he stays there until someone exercises their legal right and evicts him from that place. That is what it is like in the spiritual, what came through generationally has no right to be there, but we have to exercise our legal right, and cut it off in the generations. We need to evict that trespasser.

As I said before we do not pay the price for the sin of our parents. But think of this, a person's grandfather and father were alcoholics all their lives, but the grandson made the choice to not follow in that sin and decided not to drink. So he made the choice and was strong enough to not sin in that area. However, he knew deep down inside that he could not drink because there was a temptation that had always been there that he was suppressing and fighting because of the generational curse of alcoholism. The son, although he did not participate in the sin, was still fighting the temptation of it. That can all be released by cutting off alcohol and addiction in the generations, so he no longer has to struggle and fight. Why would you want to struggle and fight when you can be free instead?

Types of Generational Curses

There are many types of generational curses, some are physical, some are emotional, but they all have a spiritual component. As I previously mentioned, anger, alcohol, addiction, abuse (which can be physical, emotional or sexual), and drugs, act as generational curses. That is why you see them running through families in different individuals. They can also come in the form of physical ailments such as lung disorders, diseases, heart conditions, cancer and any other disease. Many suffer from generational curses that come in emotional forms, such as in depression, anxiety, fear, rejection, and unworthiness. All these are examples of generational curses that can come down through the generations.

How To Recognize Generational Curses

When you are talking to individuals whether in ministry in a church setting or in sessions of inner healing and deliverance, the Lord will often get you to ask if it runs in the family, or tell you if it is generational. This is something that when you are praying for yourself, you can also think if it runs in your family. That is a test to see if it may be generational.

I was at a church when a lady came to me the morning after a Friday night prayer time, and asked if I would still pray for her. She told me when I was going to pray for those who had asthma something rose up in her and she started to cough violently and had to leave the church and could not get prayer. The Lord told me that asthma was in her generations and was trying to prevent her from getting ministry. When I asked her if any other members of her family suffered from asthma, she told me her son did, as did her mom, and others in the family. I knew then it had to be cut off in the generations because of it running through the family blood lines. Many people still do not believe in generational curses, but I have prayed for people at times for healing, and it seems that they get well for a period of time then it reappears again without reason. So then I have gone back in and cut it off generationally and the person has become free from the generational curse from that point on. This is the difference between releasing something that needs to be cut off in the generations or not. It gives the person temporary relief but not permanent freedom.

Think of someone coming to your home and that person is offensive to you and you decide you do not want them coming over anymore, so you show them out the front door and tell them to leave. However, they still have a key to the back door and the next day you come in your front room and there they are again. You wonder how they got there, because you just kicked them out. They do not leave permanently until you take away their key that they no longer have a right to use because of Jesus. That comes by cutting them off generationally, which means you take the keys back. Jesus holds the keys to death and the grave, and everything else in our lives now because of the cross. So now we too can take the keys away from the enemy that he has been using in our lives. It is quite simple actually, but incredibly effective. I have done ministry with many people who have struggled in areas of depression, or sickness, and as soon as it is broken in the generations they are able to return to a normal life. It is amazingly powerful.

How To Cut Off Generational Curses

When the Lord or the person indicates that others in the family have suffered from this condition, it is very simple to cut the curse off in the generations. You are going to cut it off to the third and fourth generations on both the mother and father's side, because the Lord visits the iniquity of the parents back to the third and fourth generation.

Prayer

Lord in Jesus name I cut and sever all depression (or whatever you are getting from the Holy Spirit) to the third and fourth generation on my (name of person you are praying for) mother's side in Jesus name. Lord I cut all depression to the third and fourth generation on my father's side in Jesus name. Lord cut all depression generationally by the blood of the Lamb and the sword of the Spirit, in Jesus name. Cut, sever and release it all off of every part of my life, and every area it has affected in Jesus name. Lord as those generational ties are cut, place your blood in there for it never to be reconnected or reoccur again in Jesus name.

CHAPTER 7

RELEASING FALSE FOUNDATIONS

The Lord wants us to know that He has laid the foundations of the world. He created all life, and He is the foundation of all life in this world. He is also our one true and sure foundation for our life's journey on this earth.

Isaiah 51:16 - KJV

And I have put my words in thy mouth, and I have covered thee in the shadow of Mine hand, that I may plant the heavens and lay the foundations of the earth, and say unto Zion thee art My people.

What Does It Mean To Have Him As Our Foundation

Definition from "The Free Online Dictionary"

Foundation – the load bearing part of a building, a body on which all other parts rest or are overlaid, the basis on which things stand, are founded, or are supplied.

The one thing we must really grasp or understand is that Jesus is the foundation that our faith and lives are built and founded upon. He is what all things are founded through. Jesus is the foundation and solid rock which all things stand. All things are supplied and found in, and through Him. Jesus truly is the load bearing part of which the Church is built upon. Without Him the Church as a body would crumble, and without Him as our foundation our walk and lives would also crumble.

Isaiah 28:16 - KJV

Therefore thus saith the Lord God, behold I lay in Zion for a foundation a stone, a tried stone, a precious corner stone, a sure foundation, he that believeth shall not make haste.

Hebrew Translation From Key Word Study Bible

Tried - to examine, try or prove, meaning the testing verified or authenticated, the strength of the sword is verified in its testing, the stone Jesus is verified in that He has been tested and proven

Sure - appointed, established, ordained, appointed to a task and position

Jesus was laid as a "precious cornerstone", the very piece that is the stability and core of our faith and strength. The reason He was put there is that He has been tried, He was ordained, appointed, and established as exactly that. Through the testing of the cross, He was proven to be our worthy cornerstone. By the cross He proved willing to stand and do all that was required to be that very foundation that we need to build our lives upon. Without Jesus we have no foundation on which to build our faith upon. He is solid, proven, and tested. Nothing can weaken that foundation, not even death. There are no cracks in this foundation, unlike the false foundations of the world and Satan.

Jesus is the Chief Cornerstone

Ephesians 2: 19-20 - NASB

So then you are no longer strangers and aliens, but you are fellow citizens with the saints, and are of God's household, having been built upon the foundation of the apostles and prophets, Christ Jesus Himself being the cornerstone, in whom the whole building being fitted together, is growing into a holy temple in the Lord.

In the times of the bible the cornerstones were the most important parts of the stone buildings. The builder would pick four perfect stones or rocks, strong and sure that were perfect in shape to form the four corners of the building. The chief cornerstone would be the cornerstone in which the other three cornerstones would have been plumbed by. Builders would go off of the one chief cornerstone to find the other three that would be the perfect fit, for the building. Everything else would be built off of the strength of these four stones. They would hold up, and shore up the entire building. If those stones were not strong enough, big enough, or perfect in shape, then the building would be weak and unable to stand over time. That is why Jesus is called our cornerstone, our chief cornerstone. He is more than able to hold up all that is built upon Him. He is our one true and sure foundation. He is the chief cornerstone in which all else is measured to, established in, and fortified by.

So as we think of Him as our one true foundation, think of

Him kind of like the cement in this generation. He is the strongest and best quality cement that you can buy today. He is like cement that has rebar and strengthening agents in it. This cement is perfectly laid, and is able to support any size of building built upon it. No matter what storms and winds come against the building, because of the strength of the foundation, which is Jesus, that building stands. For a building's strength is only as good as the foundation that it is built upon. Jesus is that perfect foundation. There are no cracks or weaknesses in this foundation as He is a foundation of perfect quality.

What Are False Foundations?

1 Peter 2: 1-9 - NASB

Therefore putting aside all malice and all guile and hypocrisy and envy and all slander, like newborn babies, long for the pure milk of the word, that by it you may grow in respect to salvation, if you have tasted the kindness of the Lord. And coming to Him as to a living stone which has been rejected by men, but choice and precious in the sight of God, you also as living stones are being built up as a spiritual house for a holy priesthood, to offer up spiritual sacrifices acceptable to God through Jesus Christ. For this is contained in Scripture "Behold, I lay in Zion a choice stone, a precious cornerstone, and he who believes on Him will not be disappointed. This precious value, then is for you who believe; but for those who disbelieve, "The stone which the builders rejected, this became the very cornerstone, and a stone of stumbling and a rock of offense".

Some have rejected Jesus as that chief cornerstone or foundation. Some have also had foundations put in place by the world, and by the Devil before they came to the Lord. God gave me the analogy of a construction worker coming to a place to buy cement for a building. He has the choice of many different types of cement to use in his foundation. Some are cheap, but not strong, while others are quick to dry and set, but cannot hold great weight. Then there is the perfect cement that is strengthened and sure, but the construction worker decides to choose the quicker drying one that is faster to set, so he can build sooner. However, it will never hold over a long period of time the weight that is to be put on this foundation. So in time, the cement foundation he chose will crack, the building will settle and in time weaken and fall down. That is what will happen to us when we pick other false foundations of this world and the devil in which to build our lives upon.

The False Foundations Many People Build Upon

As we have established, Jesus needs to be that one true foundation that we build upon. All other foundations outside of Jesus will crack and fall apart over time. The devil offers false foundations to build things of the world upon. They too will fall for they are not strong enough to hold in times of storms or trials. Those foundations promise things that they cannot deliver; they will never hold up to what they have promised.

2nd Timothy 2:19 - KJV

Nevertheless the foundations of God standeth sure, having this seal, the Lord knoweth them that are His and let everyone that nameth the name of Christ depart from iniquity.

It says that the foundations of God standeth sure. Words with "eth" on the end mean continually. So the foundations of God continually stand sure. The foundations will not weaken over time as Jesus does not weaken over time. Nor will this foundation lose power or authority to stand, as the false foundations that the world offers will do. Jesus is a constant, unchanging, steadfast, and sure foundation. The false foundations are weak and will crack and falter over time. False foundations will never be able to stand in times of storms. We tend to build false foundations of false beliefs, false assumptions, and lies that the enemy has fed us over time. In other cases we have built false foundations because of circumstances, trauma, and pain that we have gone through. Many of these false foundations have either taken root before we knew the Lord, or through what others have done or said to us that have caused us to believe the lies about ourselves and our futures.

Think of a person that has been rejected by many people and hurt numerous times over their lifetime, especially by family members. The foundations that get built in their lives are foundations of mistrust, rejection, unworthiness, and abandonment. Those foundations are what the rest of their lives get built upon. So because of the pain, what they want or expect in their lives, is so much lower than what God's truth for their life actually is. Most times they build a much smaller and unfulfilled life than Jesus would have wanted for them because of those false foundations. So as they go forward in their life the foundations are already in place, foundations that are not built on Jesus, but false foundations. As a result when a person comes along that wants to be a part of their life and become their husband or wife, they may allow them in and marry them, but those false foundations will never allow them to build the stable life they could have had together if those false foundations were not there. All the pain and rejection that caused those false foundations to be built produced a foundation for their life that was much weaker than the one of Jesus. As a result, when they find themselves in difficult circumstances down the road, their foundation is not strong enough to bear the load and soon their lives start to fall apart. They are not standing upon the one true foundation, but on false foundations. A person can believe in Jesus but their lives, or their building, can still be built upon the false foundations of pain and lies from the past. It will not stand because Jesus was not able to be that one true foundation in the fullness He was meant to be. The Lord's heart is to remove those false foundations so that Jesus can take His place as the one true and sure foundation. The Lord does not want a part of our house built on His foundation, while still having other parts of our house built on the false foundations of the enemy. We need to have our entire home built on the one true foundation of Jesus.

Matthew 7: 24-27 - NASB

Therefore everyone then who hears these words of Mine and acts upon them may be compared to a wise man who built his house upon the rock. And the rain descended, and the floods came, and the winds blew and burst against that house, but it did not fall, because it had been founded upon the rock. And everyone who hears these words of Mine and does not act upon them will be like a foolish man who built his house upon the sand. And the rain descended, and the floods came, and the winds blew and burst against the house, and it fell, and great was its fall.

When we have false foundations in our life, it really is as if our lives are built on sand and not the solid rock of Jesus. So when the storms of life come in, we have nothing firm to stand on. The truth of the Word of God, is what our foundation should be, and to not have it will mean that the rains of life will cause what you are trying to build to come down in the storms. What is built through Jesus, on His foundation, will stand in the greatest storms, and stand the test of time.

How To Minister The Release Of False Foundations

As the Lord brings healing to so many in inner healing and deliverance in the painful areas of their lives, He does not want any false foundations left standing. He desires that they all come down. Think about it, it would be like renovating your home and fixing all the drywall, re-doing the kitchen, painting the house and re-doing the floors. You would be doing all the cosmetic work in your home, making it all new and updated, but leaving a faulty foundation. The house now looks great and is fully updated, but it still will eventually collapse if the foundation is not fixed and fortified. That is the importance of having a true, steadfast foundation in our life.

The following prayers are the prayers the Lord has led me to pray to take down all false foundations in the lives of people, so the Lord can come in and be that strong and sure foundation.

Prayer

Lord Jesus please forgive me for placing hope in false foundations and not in You. For you are the only one true foundation. Lord by the blood of the Lamb and the sword of the Spirit every false foundation is covered in the blood, nullified, broken, and loosed. Lord by the blood of Jesus, and the power of the Holy Spirit, and by the very hand of

God, every false foundation comes down in Jesus name. Lord cause every false foundation to break apart and be removed by your hand Lord in Jesus name. In the name of Jesus, Lord establish in her/him (name) the one true foundation in its place which is you Jesus. Jesus you are the one true, tried and sure foundation in which my/their life can stand. So Lord establish yourself as that foundation where every lie, every deceit, and every false belief system has built foundations in the past. Lord I ask you now to be that precious cornerstone in Jesus name.

CHAPTER 8

THE POWER OF RELEASING ENMITY

Another area where so much inner healing and deliverance is done is enmity. Understanding enmity is key as inner healing and deliverance cannot be done in its fullness until enmity is removed.

What Is Enmity?

Enmity means ill will, avoidance, deep seated dislike, hostility, being at opposition with, and even hatred. Enmity can be either open or concealed in a person's life. It is also rancor which is brooding over a wrong. So as you can see, enmity can be from something as small as ill will, avoidance, or dislike, to complete hatred, and being at complete opposition to someone. If enmity remains oppressing someone it acts like a cavern or a crevasse with the person with whom they are at enmity with. It is like one person is on one side of the crevasse, with the other on the other side, with no way across. There is no way to even forgive the person as enmity acts as a breach with no access to what or who a person is at enmity with.   You can be at enmity with a person, with God, and you can even be at enmity with yourself.

Genesis 3:9-15 - AMP

And the Lord God called to Adam and said to him, where are you? I heard the sound of you (walking) in the garden, and I was afraid because I was naked and I hid myself. And He said, who told you that you were naked? Have you eaten of the tree of which I commanded you that you should not eat? And the man said, the woman whom You gave to be with me, she gave me (fruit) from the tree, and I ate. And the Lord God said to the woman, what is this you have done? And the woman said, the serpent beguiled (cheated, outwitted, and deceived) me and I ate. And the Lord said to the serpent, because you have done this, you are cursed above all (domestic) animals and above every (wild) living thing of the field: upon your belly you shall go, and you shall eat dust (and what it contains) all the days of your life. And I will put enmity between you and the woman, and between your offspring and her offspring: He will bruise and tread your head underfoot, and you will lie in wait and bruise His heel. (Gal 4:4)

Enmity came in first between man and God because Adam hid himself from God and for the first time he was avoiding Him. He was brooding over the wrong that he knew he had committed. He had never avoided God before.

When Adam was asked who told him to eat the fruit of the tree he pointed the finger at Eve. The moment Adam did that he put enmity between him and Eve. Now enmity had also come in between man and woman. There was now hostility and ill will between Adam and Eve. When Adam blamed Eve, he held up Eve as the opposition. Enmity always blames others and never sees its own responsibility in circumstances. Ill will, bitterness, and enmity now had crept into the Garden of Eden. The crevasse was now being put in place between man and woman, man and God, and man and the serpent.

God Tells Us With Whom We Are In Enmity

Now notice in the Bible in Genesis in verse 15 God says, "and I will put enmity between you and the woman and between your offspring and her offspring". Because of the sin of Adam and Eve the Lord put enmity (dislike, ill will, opposition, hostility and hatred) between the serpent, or Satan, man, and all the offspring to follow. God drew the battle lines in the Garden of Eden and showed us who we were to be at enmity or at opposition to, the devil. Too many times we seem to be at enmity with each other, and with God Himself, and not with the one God declared with whom we should be at enmity with. God made it pretty clear that it is the devil himself we are to be in enmity with and him alone. We need to remember who we are at war with, not each other. So many in inner healing and deliverance have enmity with other people, and many have enmity with God Himself. How can we then receive healing from God when we are at enmity with Him. Clearly that is not our opposition, so it has to leave. Some are even at enmity with themselves due to self-hatred and how they see themselves as unworthy and rejected. That has to be released for them to be able to see themselves as Jesus sees them, so they may receive the healing they need. Enmity acts as that crevasse keeping us from the healing we need.

Jesus Destroyed All Enmity On The Cross

Ephesians 2:13-18 - AMP

But now in Christ Jesus, you who once were (so) far away, through (by, in) the blood of Christ have been brought near. For He is (Himself) our peace (our bond of unity and harmony). He has made us both (Jew and Gentile) one (body), and has broken down (destroyed, abolished) the hostile dividing wall between us. By abolishing in His (own crucified) flesh the enmity (caused by) the Law with its decrees and ordinances (which He annulled); that He from the two might create in Himself one new man (one new quality of humanity out of the two) so making peace. And (He designed) to reconcile to God both (Jew and Gentile, united) in a single body by means of His cross, thereby killing the mutual enmity and bringing the feud to an end. And He came and preached the glad tidings of peace to you who were afar off and (peace) to those who were near. (Isa 57:19) For it is through Him that we both (whether far off or near) now have an introduction (access) by one (Holy) Spirit to the Father (So we are able to approach Him).

Notice in this passage that there was a hostile dividing wall between Jews and Gentiles, in other words, enmity. That hostile dividing wall of enmity had now been destroyed on the cross. The cross destroyed, abolished, and slayed the enmity between not only man and man, but between man and God that the Law or the devil put in place. It said that His body on the cross, killed, slayed, or destroyed enmity once and for all. The problem is mankind does not fully understand that, and the devil does not want us to see that Jesus already has victory over all enmity. The enemy is always causing separation and division. It is as if he is hammering a wedge, or space (opposition, animosity, hostility, ill will) in the lives of people and families. God always showed it to me as a hammer hammering a wedge into a big log. The enemy with swings of a big hammer pounds down the wedge into the log blow by blow. With each swing the split goes deeper, and the crevasse grows larger, making the split in the log bigger and bigger till the log is completely split in two. That is how enmity works in our lives. The cross took out that wedge that the devil put in. It says in the Bible in God's Word, "He is the repairer of the breach". That is what Jesus did through the cross. We need to understand this truth so that we can understand what is being done in Inner Healing and Deliverance in the releasing of enmity.

Enmity Is Always Growing and Acts As A Root System

Enmity is never stagnant, it is always growing. That crevasse or breach is always getting larger. It may have started as ill will or avoidance, but it grows to strong dislike, then to hostility, and then to hatred. It is always growing and expanding in our lives.

God has always shown me that enmity is like a root system in our lives. It Is easily undetected and grows underground. As a result, we do not always know how deep or wide enmity goes. The devil is always looking to grow that root system deeper into one's life, into a church, or even into a city or community. Because Jesus is the repairer of the breach, and took it upon Himself and destroyed all breaches or enmity on the cross, He is the only one that can pull all enmity out, and release it from a person's life.

How To Release Enmity In A Person's Life

In ministry through the gifts of the Holy Spirit, the Spirit reveals to you that there is either enmity in your life, or in the life of the person you are ministering to. The next step is to identify who the enmity is against. It may be against God, a person, or maybe even ourselves. Ask the Lord to give you the eyes to see ears to hear and heart to understand where there is enmity in your life. The Holy Spirit will then show you or the person you are ministering to, who you are at enmity with. Sometimes it may be one or two people, or ourselves, or even God but ask the Lord to show you who it is. Next ask Jesus to show you how it has affected your life, relationships, and even your walk with God. Once the Holy Spirit has explained it to you, or anyone you are ministering to, the Lord is able to go in and release all enmity. In the spirit I see it as Him going in and pulling all enmity out by the roots. An easy way to minister in this area is to say "in Jesus name Lord pull out by the roots all enmity in that person's life". The thing

that destroyed all enmity on that cross was the love of
Jesus that He brought when He laid down His life for each
one of us. Love covers a multitude of sin, and the love of
our Savior truly releases all the enmity. For in the Bible in
the King James version of Ephesians 2:13-18 it says
"Having abolished in his flesh the enmity", so you can see
He has abolished all enmity that came into the garden
through sin so many years ago. He did this by crucifying
His flesh on the cross.

Situations Where Enmity Is Usually Found

Releasing enmity in a person's life has a profound effect.
It truly allows them to proceed on in their ministry
because the enmity in their lives truly acted like a giant
crevasse that prevented them from going forward.
Praying this works amazingly well in people having marital
problems, family disputes, and people having a hard time
getting closer to the Lord. It also works well for people
who have had a hard time receiving love from the Lord
because of how they see themselves, or God. In any
relationship that seems to have a large amount of
animosity, or where two people are at opposition to each
other, usually enmity is involved. I have seen marriages
reconciled where there was once enmity. Where there
was once that crevasse, there is now a coming together
where forgiveness and reconciliation could finally occur. I
have seen people who have had enmity released are now
able to go forward in their walk with God for the first time.

They are now able to truly receive the love and grace of a loving Father that enmity once prevented them from receiving. For how can we go forward in our walk with God and in our relationships with Him, if we have avoidance, or are at opposition with Him in any area of our life? Check and ask the Holy Spirit if there is enmity in your life. He will let you know, and then He will remove it. For enmity will always hold you back in your journey with the Lord.

Prayer

This is an example of how to minister in releasing enmity. First bind all according to Ephesians 6:12 and release His anointing and the gifts of the Spirit. Give Jesus Lordship over your prayers and your time with Him.

Lord I ask you to show and reveal to me where I have any enmity in the name of Jesus. Lord I ask you give me the eyes to see ears to hear and heart to understand how it has affected my life in Jesus name. Pause and wait for Him to speak to you in this place. Give Him time to speak. Lord in Jesus name, go in and pull out by the roots all enmity in my life in Jesus name. (Or name the person you are ministering to) Lord all enmity is pulled out by the roots, enmity to God, to man and to myself all goes in the name of Jesus. Lord every bit comes out, pull it all out by your hand God. Lord thank you that all enmity was slain on the cross and that now you are releasing it all from my life in

Jesus name. Lord it says in your Word, You are the repairer of the breach. So Lord where any breach or enmity was, Jesus, fill that crevasse with your love, your blood, and the power of the Holy Spirit in Jesus name. Lord let your love fill and heal that place where enmity once was in the name of Jesus. Restore all that enmity has robbed me of, in Jesus name. (If the Lord gives you anything else to remove that came in with the enmity, then pray to release it now as well, for example unworthiness, rejection etc.) Lord I thank you that you heal and seal every area of my heart in your blood where all enmity once was in Jesus name.

CHAPTER 9

THE POWER OF TRUTH

We underestimate the power of the truth of God to set us free when praying for ourselves or for others. Truth in itself is power, as it is the power to uncover all that is false and to reveal the truth which sets us free from the lies of the enemy.

What God's Truth Means

Greek Translation From Key Note Study Bible

Greek meaning - What is not concealed but open and known, purity from all error or falsehood, declaring the existence and will of the one true God. Jesus is the truth; He is the teacher of all divine truth. He declares or reveals divine truth. Truth is genuine, opposite of false or pretend, upright in heart, and it is tested as genuine. The Spirit of truth declares or reveals divine truth in all things.

What we also need to remember is that the devil is the complete opposite of all that is written above. Everything he weaves in our lives is also the complete opposite of that. We as the Church of Jesus Christ need to truly know the immense power of the truth in our lives, and in our situations and how it exposes the works of the enemy, to set us free.

John 14:6 - NASB

Jesus said to him, I am the way, and the truth, and the life; no man comes to the Father, but through Me.

Jesus is truth itself. Everything about Him and what He

speaks and teaches is genuine, true, and **has no error or falsehood**. He Himself has no error or falsehood in that He has been tested by the cross and found to be genuine and true, the bearer of divine truth. Truth in its purest form gives life and freedom, and that is what Jesus came to this earth to do to give life and freedom to each one of us in every situation. He came to destroy the works of the devil.

This is why the enemy spends as much time as he does trying to cover up the truth in every area of our lives. He understands the power of truth to set us free. The divine truth of God about us or our situation will cause all that the enemy has built in our life to fall apart and be dismantled. It cannot stand under the truth of God.

John 18:37 - NASB

Pilate therefore said to Him, "So You are King?" Jesus answered, "you say that I am a King. For this I have been born and for this I have come into the world, to bear witness to the truth. Everyone who is of the truth hears My voice."

Jesus comes into our lives to show us the truth, first of all who He is, the Messiah and that He holds the keys to death and the grave, and that we are saved through Him. He then proceeds to show us His truth in all things. The truth of who He is and His promises, but also to expose all the lies of the enemy in our lives through His truth. His truth is like a big flashlight that shines into the darkness where the enemy tries to hide the lies in, hoping that we will stumble around long enough to become discouraged, resulting in us no longer looking for that truth and the freedom it brings. That is why the Lord shines that light. His light goes into those dark places that are cloaked in the lies and schemes of the enemy so that He can show us the truth and cause the lies to fall away so we can be free.

You see the enemy always tries to make the lies seem so big and insurmountable, unable to be changed in any way. When the Lord shines the light of truth upon them, they are exposed in the true light and we see how small they really are. Many times in ministry, people will see the size of the obstacles they are facing just shrink before their eyes after the Lord shines His light of truth. Lies only have the power that we allow them to have, or to the degree that the enemy has oppressed us in that area. Jesus came to reveal the truth in all things so that we would not fall into error or be deceived by the enemy.

Truth will always stand the test of time, but error and falsehood will always collapse and be removed by the hand of God. That is why it is so powerful and why we need to pray as a Church for God's truth to be revealed in all things in every area of our lives, as well as in every situation we face.

John 16:13 - NASB

But, when He the Spirit of truth comes, He will guide you into all the truth, for He will not speak on His own initiative, but whatever He hears He will speak, and He will disclose to you what is to come.

The Enemy Puts Fear and Enmity Between Us And The Truth

The enemy knows the power of truth. Truth has the power to set one free, so, as a result the enemy spends a lot of time trying to keep us from the truth at all costs. One of his strategies is to put enmity between us and the truth that will set us free.

John 8:31 - NASB

Jesus therefore was saying to those Jews who had believed Him, if you abide in My word, then you are truly disciples of Mine, and you shall know the truth, and the truth shall set you free.

The Holy Spirit will lead you and speak to you about all truth in your life; you only need to ask. So many times we have fear of the truth, so we do not want to ask about the truth in our situation. Who do you think causes us to fear the truth? The devil does, as he is the one who really fears the truth and he understands the freedom it brings. His tactic is to simply place fear and enmity between us and the truth so we will no longer desire to seek it out, thus keeping us in bondage. It says in the Bible in 2nd Timothy 1:7 "God did not give us a spirit of fear, but of love, power, and a sound mind". The enemy uses fear and enmity because he needs to keep us from the truth at all costs, because he fears our freedom. He fears the freedom of the Church moving in complete power. Fear causes us to turn from the truth and the freedom it brings.   Enmity also works powerfully against our lives, hindering us in discovering the truth in the areas that we have oppression in. Enmity and the power it has over our life causes us to avoid the truth. The enemy then increases the enmity to the truth in our lives till we are actually at opposition to the very truth that will set us free. As a result, we turn away from the truth of God, embracing the lie. We end up seeing the truth as something we should avoid. The lie that the enemy spins says it will harm us, and keep us in bondage rather than setting us free. The lie says the truth will only hurt us or cause us more pain. Enmity causes us to believe the lie that covers the truth. Enmity truly buries the truth in an even greater way.

The enemy knows he cannot alter truth. The truth cannot be changed, so he spends much time disguising all truth, covering it up with lies, fears, and enmity so we will never find it. He knows the power of truth sets us free. As previously mentioned the devil is the one that really fears truth and the freedom it brings. We need to learn to pray out all fear, enmity and barriers to the truth as it affects our life. The truth is where all freedom is. Truth brings understanding, wisdom, and direction. Pray for it, seek after it, and desire to understand the revelation of truth in each of your situations that you are going through.   Pray and ask the Lord in Jesus name to release a spirit of revelation, wisdom, and understanding of His truth in what you are going through. You will be amazed at how powerful the truth really is in your life.

John 8:42-44 - AMP

Jesus said to them, if God were your Father, you would love Me, for I proceeded forth and have come from God, for I have not even come on My own initiative, but He sent Me. Why do you not understand what I am saying? It is because you cannot hear My word. You are of your father the devil, and you want to do the desires of your father. He was a murderer from the beginning, and does not stand in the truth because there is no truth in him. Whenever he speaks a lie, he speaks from his own nature; for he is a liar, and the father of lies.

God is the father of all truth and the devil is the father of all lies.

So as the scripture states there is not one ounce of truth in him, none. Everything of the enemy is false, has error, and has not one bit of truth in it. So why at times do we still listen to what the devil has to say? Why do we allow him to speak to the point that we have listened to so much of his lies that we begin to see those lies as truth? It is alright to interrupt him, and command him to be quiet in Jesus name. Pray that you reject his lies, and will not receive any of them into your heart. Do not let him speak his entire lie out, for then you are battling the entire lie that he is trying to drop into your heart, not just a couple of words. We need to be kind to each other, but not to the enemy. Command him to be quiet and then cover the words he spoke in the blood of Jesus and ask the Lord to remove them from your mind and heart, in Jesus name. Ask the Lord to expose the lies of the enemy and to remove them in Jesus name. Then ask God to deposit His truth into your heart.

Psalm 117:2 - NASB

For His lovingkindness is great toward us; And the truth of the Lord is everlasting, praise be to the Lord.

The truth of Jesus and His word endures forever, it will never pass away. It is without end. It says in the Bible in the Word of God that the gifts of God will come to an end, but the Word will never pass away. The Word is complete truth. Jesus and the Word of God is the one thing we can hang onto, and depend on eternally. God is also not the author of confusion, the enemy is. That is another tactic the enemy uses. He uses confusion to cover the truth, making it harder to sort out what is of God, what is of you, and what is of him. God's truth will reveal all the lies, and release all confusion. Ask the Lord to release all confusion from your mind and heart, and to release His Spirit of truth to you to speak truth and to guide you in your situation. Ask Him to give you the eyes to see, the ears to hear, and the heart to understand what the truth is that you are seeking.

2nd Corinthians 13:8 - NASB

For we can do nothing against the truth, but only for the

truth.

What a revelation of the truth this scripture truly is. **The truth itself and about your situation, or about you can never be removed or taken away. It can only be covered up. As you can do nothing against the truth, it is unalterable**. Truth is like a buried treasure that the enemy has covered up under years of lies, pain and hurt. But when the Lord comes in with His light of truth, He reveals where that treasure is and digs up the truth that has been buried under the rubble for so long. So when we open that box, the truth truly becomes a treasure beyond any measure. It really does set us free. Jesus Himself is the pearl of great price, the greatest treasure of all, and the treasure of divine truth.

Jesus is waiting for us to ask Him what the truth of our situation really is. Nothing pleases the heart of the Father more than to show His children the truth of their identity, and of what He is able to do for them in every situation they face. Let Jesus expose that treasure of truth in every area of your life. Any fear, enmity, or confusion to the truth came from the enemy, not from God. It was the enemy's way of keeping you from being free.

Prayer For Releasing Enmity and Fear To The Truth of God

These are the prayers to pray when releasing all enmity, fear, and barriers that the enemy placed between you and the truth. If you are unsure if you have that in any area of your life, simply ask the Lord to show you, in Jesus name, if there are any areas where you have fear or enmity to the truth. The enemy also tries to put in fear and enmity to the Word of God, which is the purest form of truth. Some will have found an inability to spend time in the word, or the understanding and belief that it is the infallible Word of God. Removing the fear and enmity to the Word, then releases them to be able to go in and receive from the Word of God whatever it is that the Lord desires to give them.

Prayer

Lord I ask You in Jesus name to remove all enmity to the truth in every area of my life. Lord pull out all enmity by the roots with your hand God that kept me from your truth, and the freedom it brings in Jesus name. Lord, all enmity comes out, in the name of Jesus. Lord it says you are the repairer of the breach, so Lord repair every breach to your truth through your blood, your love, and the power of the Holy Spirit, in Jesus name.

Lord I also ask you to bind and lose all fear, confusion, and all barriers that block access to your truth, in Jesus name. All fear and confusion is cut, severed, broken, and loosed by the blood of the lamb and the sword of the spirit, in Jesus name. Release it all Lord, and give me the eyes to see, the ears to hear, and the heart to understand your truth.

Lord, I ask you to shine your light into the darkness and show me Your truth in my situation in Jesus name. Remove every lie and deception that buried the truth and my freedom, in Jesus name. Lord, release a spirit of revelation and wisdom about your truth and guide my steps. I release your truth to set me free, and to guide me in all things in my life, in Jesus name.

Releasing Enmity To The Truth of The Word of God

Lord I ask you to release all enmity to the Word of God in Jesus name. Lord pull it all out by the roots, with your hand God, pull all enmity out in Jesus name. Lord it says you are a repairer of the breach, so Lord repair every breach to Your Word, in Jesus name. Fill the breach with your blood and the power of the Holy Spirit. Remove all confusion of the Word that came in through that breach, in Jesus name. Lord, I ask you to release a spirit of revelation, wisdom, and understanding, and that Your Holy Spirit be my teacher and guide through Your Word. Let Your Word be a source of life to me and a compass to point to all truth, in Jesus name.

CHAPTER 10
CURSE WORDS

Our words have the power to edify, teach, and exhort. On the other hand, words have the power to tear down, destroy and make people feel worthless. We need to understand our words, when received by an individual's heart, can truly affect the way they see themselves and God. As God's Church we need to understand the power of negative words and the damaging affect it has in people's lives.

Proverbs 16:24 - NASB

Pleasant words are like a honeycomb, sweetness to the soul and healing to the bones.

The words that edify and build us up are sweet and bring edification, peace and health to the body, mind, and soul. It builds us up and helps us to see God and ourselves in His truth that we are loved, important, valued and cherished.

How Words Curse Our Lives

Psalm 52:2 - NASB

The tongue devises mischiefs like a sharp razor, working deceitfully.

Proverbs 11:9 - NASB

With his mouth the godless man destroys his neighbor, but by knowledge the righteous are delivered.

Proverbs 12:18 - AMP

There are those who speak rashly like the piercing of a sword, but the tongue of the wise brings healing.

Proverbs 18:21 - NASB

Death and life are in the power of the tongue, and those who love it will eat its fruits.

These are powerful scriptures regarding the power of the words we speak. Our words will either bring life or death to a person. They will either build up or tear down. When we use words that tear someone down it is like we are using swords that are razor sharp to cut into the very heart of a person. We do not often think of this before we speak, but we should. Notice the first scripture talks about how words can be used like a sharp razor working deceitfully. Who do you think uses words like that in other people's life? The devil, of course, uses those words. He uses the words of hate, anger, lies, bitterness, envy and deceit to bring destruction into another person's life.

The greatest battles that we wage against the enemy are thoughts from the devil and the words that others speak against us. When we dwell long enough on the destructive words people say, we allow them to drop into our heart, and they now become a part of how we see ourselves. Those words that were lies of the enemy now become our truths. The enemy has used these words to curse our lives because we have believed in what they represented. That is why we must take every thought captive. We also need to take what others say about us captive, and not allow the words that were meant to tear us down to drop into our hearts. Most people that say destructive things are really speaking out of a place of hurt and pain in their own lives. For out of the mouth comes the abundance of the heart.

In some cases, the words that are spoken to us come with a spirit behind them with the full intent to do as much damage as possible. When I have talked to people that I have done prayer ministry with, they have even mentioned how those words have defiled them, and cut them to the core, deeper than other words have. That is because those words did not come from someone's flesh, they came from a spirit with the power of the devil behind it. That is why those words cut so much deeper and have a purpose behind them to bring destruction in an area of a person's life. They were not just only the idle words of an individual that the enemy was able to use because of a person's carelessness. These words were planned and set in place by the enemy to cause harm and to bring despair. They were spoken to put a person in a particular bondage. In most cases these curse words have blocked a person's walk and intimacy with God because of the lies they now believe about themselves or the Lord.

Proverbs 15:4 - NASB

A soothing tongue is a tree of life, but perversion in it crushes the spirit.

When the words of a person are defiled with perverseness and then spoken to an individual, it breaks a person's spirit. It literally changes them, breaks them down and causes much pain and heartache. In severe cases, it will cause them to completely change the direction of their lives. These words will cause them to give up dreams and desires that the Lord had put in them.

How To Have Victory Over Curse Words

In cases where it is the idle words of people that were not thinking, or speaking from their own jealousy or pain, it is fairly easy to deal with. Every person can deal with them on their own. First of all, take every thought captive as the Bible teaches. When someone says something negative to you that would make you feel less about yourself, stop for a moment and see if that word is in agreement with what the Word of God says about you. If it is not, then pray in your head or out loud, Lord I rebuke those words in Jesus name, I cover them in the blood and I receive none of them into my heart or spirit in the name of Jesus. You do not have to receive any of those words that were meant to tear you down. You can rebuke them, nullify them with the blood of Jesus, and ask the Lord to take them away. This way they never get to the point that they will curse your life, or affect you in any way. That is why God tells us to think on things that are lovely, pure, kind, and gentle. If we are dwelling over the negative words of others, we run the danger of allowing them to drop into our hearts, resulting in the words acting as a curse in our lives.

Now for those words that have dropped into our hearts, causing us to believe the lies that someone spoke about us. Or for those words that came from the enemy with the intent to hurt, ridicule, and cause heartache, they too, through Jesus and the power of the blood shed on the cross, can be broken off our lives. He took every word on Himself that would ever be spoken against us. Jesus took all the pain, shame and guilt of all those words as well onto Himself. He took it all and the victory is already ours. Once again we just have to apply that victory and authority in our lives that Jesus gave us through the cross. Every word that was spoken that has cut us and sliced through our hearts and souls causing us so much pain, the Lord is able to remove. Jesus is able to remove the words and the effects of them, replacing them with the truth and removing the lie. He is also able to extract the poison of those words that seemed to poison our hearts and minds really against ourselves.

Prayer

In each case where the words that others spoke against us, out of hurt, fear or bitterness, or the words that came with the intent to wound and cause heartache from the devil, the prayer is the same. Many times the enemy will use the pain of others around you, especially family members, to hurt, wound and send those sharp razors like swords into our hearts. The Lord however is able to nullify every one of those words and bring healing to your heart. Just pray as follows:

Lord in Jesus name every curse word that was spoken against (you or anyone you may be ministering to) is covered in the blood of Jesus, nullified, broken, and loosed off of my/their mind, heart, body, and spirit in the name of Jesus. Lord all poisons, lies, and deceptions that entered through those words are also covered in the blood of Jesus nullified, broken, and loosed off of my/their mind, heart, and body in Jesus name. Lord release it all now in the name of Jesus. Lord I ask you to give me/them the truth about my/their situation, Lord. Speak to their hearts and plant in their heart the truth of who they are. Give them the eyes to see, the ears to hear, and the heart to understand and receive that truth. Thank you Lord Jesus that every curse word spoken against me/them is nullified by the blood of the lamb, in Jesus name.

Make sure that, whether it is for you or another person that you let the Lord spend enough time to remove all the pain that came in with those curse words. He may also get you to releases pain, trauma, sorrow, grief, and loss, or anything else that those words brought into your life. The Holy Spirit will lead you whether there is more to release due to the words spoken. Always give the person time to hear the truth about who they are or their situation, and the reasons behind why those words were spoken against them. It will bring understanding and complete healing in that situation for them or for yourself.

CHAPTER 11

THE POWER OF ACCUSATIONS IN OUR LIVES

The power of accusations is incredible whether raised against churches, pastors, families, or individuals.

An accusation is a charge or claim that someone has done something wrong. It is a charge of shortcoming or error, or a formal charge of wrongdoing. We just need to understand how accusations made against us have profound effects in our lives, our churches, and the lives of the ones we care for.

Revelation 12:10-12 - NASB

And I heard a loud voice in heaven saying, now the salvation and the power, and the Kingdom of our God and the authority of His Christ have come, for the accuser of our brethren has been thrown down, who accuses them before our God day and night. And they overcame him because of the blood of the Lamb and because of the word of their testimony, and they did not love their life even to death. For this reason, rejoice, O heavens and you who dwell in them. Woe to the earth and the sea, because the devil has come down to you having great wrath, knowing that he has only a short time.

How Accusations Work

We know that the devil is the accuser of the brethren.

The enemy has two major weapons. We tend to know more about the first, lies and deceit. We tend to recognize these ones because the church overall has more knowledge regarding this and how it works. As a result, we tend to guard better against this weapon. However, the one we know less about in regards to how it affects us is the weapon of accusations. It is one we rarely guard ourselves against. We do not realize how accusations rob us, steal from us, weaken us, and make us ineffective. Why would the enemy accuse us both day and night if it was not a powerful weapon? First of all it stops us from going forward in life. Remember Jesus and the apostles tell us life and death is in the tongue. Jesus intercedes on our behalf to the Father and the devil accuses us before the Father. One builds up, and one tears down, just like curse words. The Lord uses our prayers of intercession to do His will on this earth, but the enemy uses our accusations to do the opposite. He uses it to come against the will of the Lord in people's lives. The accusations of the saints of God against each other are even more powerful than those who do not believe in God. Words of accusation that are spoken by believers work more powerfully against us because believers are filled with the power of the Holy Spirit. The enemy understands this and loves to use the accusations of God's people. Most will not even understand what they are being used for which is why we need to know how to counter those accusations. We are surrounded by the power of words. God spoke the world into existence. The Word became flesh, so you see the spoken word is so much more powerful than we ever knew. So remember the Lord intercedes according to the will of God, but the enemy makes accusations against the will of God. Accusations are a key for the enemy to cause man to not walk in the fullness of what God has for them, thus watering down the power of the Church. If the enemy can cause people in a church to accuse each other, think how much it will deplete the power and effectiveness of that church. Accusations will usher in strife, division, enmity, and discord.

Matthew 18:19-20 - NASB Power of the Prayer of Agreement

Again I say to you, that if two of you agree on earth about anything that they may ask, it shall be done for them by My Father who is in heaven. For where two or three have gathered together in My name I am there in their midst.

So we know the principle of going before God and the power of a prayer of agreement made between two believers. It is one of the most powerful prayers that we can pray. When we make accusations we come in a prayer of agreement with the enemy over another person's life. As Jesus is always looking for those whom He can use to bring through prayer the Father's will, the devil is always looking for those he can use to bring about his will through accusations and lies. The Holy Spirit is looking for those who will pray on behalf of the Father, the enemy is looking for those who will agree with him. Criticism, judgement, slander, gossip, and accusations cause us to come in a form of agreement with the enemy.

Now we all make accusations at times, the odd comment, but it is when we are continually speaking out against an individual, church, leader, or family member that those accusations are used for destruction. When we continually do this the enemy is able to attach spirits to our words to come against us, and do damage to others, their lives, or their ministries. Accusations in the spirit stop the progression forward in individual lives, families, and churches. The enemy uses those accusations to come against us, or our churches when it can do the most damage. He always waits till the cost would be the greatest. The enemy holds his deck of cards close to his chest, and will use whichever hand he needs that will cost us the most. However, with God, spiritual knowledge on this allows us to break through the power those accusations may have caused and release it from our lives.

Accusations Test Our Integrity

In the Bible in the first chapter in the Book of Job, God is honoring Job. God was saying he was blameless, upright, and God fearing. He turned away from evil. Now Satan makes an accusation against Job. He basically tells God that the only reason he is good is because God has given him wealth, goods, cattle, and protection. He stated that anyone would be faithful if you gave all of that to them. Satan was basically questioning Job's integrity. When an accusation is raised, it must be answered. God was allowing Satan to test Job. Job's integrity and faith were being tested and Job passed the test. The accusations of the enemy cost Job much, but because of the integrity of Job and his belief in God, all was restored two fold. We need to see how the accusations against Job cost him so much. We also need to understand Job did not even know the accusations that were being made against him. Many times, we do not know the accusations made against us, our church, or our family. We must rely on the Holy Spirit to lead us and to keep an ear to any accusations raised against ourselves, or our church, so that the Holy Spirit can then lead us to pray.

Tests of Integrity Come When Accusations Are Raised

Now when accusations are raised there will always be tests of integrity. They are generally not big tests like Job endured, but they are small and harder to recognize. Nevertheless, your integrity will be tested. We need to ask the Lord to grant us the grace that when a time of testing comes in accusations, the Holy Spirit will lead us to do what is right. Now when we deal with accusations there is a way to pray that will allow us to have victory over them. We must remember that all accusations usually will have a small thread of truth, although it be very small, that thread still exists in what we are being accused of.

Matthew 5:25 - AMP

Come to terms with your accuser while you are on the way

traveling with him, lest your accuser hand you over to the judge, and the judge to the guard and you be put in prison.

You are better to face your accuser (the enemy or a person) and ask God for forgiveness in any way you may have offended them, hurt them, or done something wrong. Remember there is usually a small thread of truth, or a perception of that truth. In other words, someone could have mistaken what you did for something else. You need to recognize that and ask for forgiveness, as it says in the Bible blessed be the peace maker. Many times the other party may not change their stance or opinion, in which case that is now their issue and God will hold them accountable for their opinion or stance. You have done what God has asked you to do. You have asked for forgiveness and extended your hand to make things right, so you now leave it with God. One time I had one person accusing me of many things that were not true, and continued to accuse me of many things I did not do. I wanted so much to defend myself, but the Lord told me to be quiet. He told me this was not about me, and that I would do more harm if I spoke out, because the enemy would use the words I spoke out against me down the road. So I kept quiet and said nothing and just asked if the person would forgive me, and if I had hurt them in any way that I was sorry. I told them that I cared about them and I was sorry they felt that way. By keeping quiet, I added no fuel to the fire and kept my integrity before God. I had asked for forgiveness so the enemy had no legal foothold to use, and I just released the person to God and went on. It truly is the best way to handle things. Jesus Himself when being accused of blasphemy and so much more by His accusers just kept quiet and said nothing. He is our example of how to handle the words of others. Many times because of people's pain in their lives they can take something you did or say to mean something else. Then they come and accuse you of something you never did. This is why accusations at times are really made through misunderstandings. Asking for forgiveness if it was taken the wrong way diffuses it, and shuts out the enemy. Some instances are more complex and that is why in all things, get the leading of the Lord. He spoke very clearly to me as to what I was to do and it instantly diffused the situation. Maybe there are accusations going around about you. They are not true, but they have an effect on you, your job, or your family. Remember there is usually a small thread of truth to those accusations. It may be that what you did was taken the wrong way. Still go to God and ask Him to forgive you for anything that you may have said or done that could have been perceived that way. Then ask the Lord to release anything you may have done or said that caused that person pain, in Jesus name. This is about you being free from the power of accusations in your life and the Lord will deal with the other person.

How To Nullify the Power of Accusations In The Spirit

To release the power of accusations that have been spoken out against you, you will also want to pray against them and nullify their affect. You also need to bind them, forbidding them to spread gossip and to slander your name or the Church. That is what the intent of the accusation is meant to do. Accusations bring slander, gossip and backbiting amongst people. They bring in strife, division, bitterness, and resentment. They are meant to cause further conflict in your family, church, or home. That is why you need to meet them head on and not run from them. For not dealing with them can only prolong the problem, causing it to fester and grow.

Prayer is powerful when dealing with this type of situation whether individually, as a ministry, or as a church. The first thing you want to do is to bind all strife division, bitterness, resentment, slander, gossiping, and backbiting from spreading in your church, or in the community. Then you will pray for the accusations themselves to be nullified in the blood of Jesus. The following is an example of a prayer you could pray for accusations that have been released against you, your church, or community.

Prayer

Lord, I ask for forgiveness, for anything I have done or said or anything that has hurt anyone or given the appearance of this being the intent of my heart. Lord, please forgive me of anything that I have said or done that could have caused this accusation and pain. Lord, in Jesus name, I bind and forbid any further spreading of strife, division, separation, slander, gossiping or backbiting in Jesus name. Lord I bind it and forbid it to move among the congregation or my family in Jesus name. Shut down every spirit of slander and accusation that was meant to bring harm to me, the church or my family in Jesus name. Lord every accusation made against me is covered in the blood, nullified, broken, and loosed and goes back to the dust of the earth from where it came from. Lord in Jesus name I bind any other ear from receiving this lie in Jesus name. All accusations fall on deaf ears, to be heard no more or taken in as truth in the name of Jesus. Lord I am sorry for anything that I have done or not done, said or not said that has added to this situation in Jesus name. Lord cover all of this in the blood, nullify it, and break it off of me and everyone else involved by the blood of the Lamb and the sword of the Spirit in Jesus name. Lord I release your truth and spirit of reconciliation and unity into this entire situation, in the name of Jesus.

CHAPTER 12

THE BLESSINGS AND CURSES OF DEUTERONOMY

In the Bible in Deuteronomy 28 it talks about the blessings and curses the people would receive if they were obedient or disobedient to God. In the Old Testament you received the blessings if you were obedient to God and did what the Law said. You would also however, receive the curses if you were disobedient to the Law. So in the Old Testament, or Old Covenant, the blessings of God depended upon whether you were obedient or not. Contrarily the New Covenant, or the New Testament is based on grace not obedience, yet so many Christians are still living partially under the curse or Law. We no longer live under the Law, but the enemy still tries to release the curses found in Deuteronomy into our lives.

Galatians 3:10-11 - NASB

For as many as are of the works of the Law are under a curse; for it is written, Cursed is everyone who does not abide by all things written in the Book of the Law, to perform them. Now that no one is justified by the Law before God is evident; for, the righteous man shall live by faith.

It is a gift from God that we no longer have to live by the Law, because we have been justified through grace by what Jesus did on the cross. He redeemed us from the Law and the curse that the Law brought. Not one of us can live totally free from sin. Our faith is not conditional on what we do, or do not do. Our salvation is a gift through our faith and belief in what Jesus did on the cross. The Law pointed to sin and our desperate need for a savior, and the cross pointed to redemption and freedom from our sin. God no longer judges us by the Law as in the Old Testament, but the devil however, would love to bring these curses upon our lives. To be cursed is to be separated from God, but we do not live a life separated from Him. Through the cross we now have a relationship with the very God from whom we used to be separated. In this relationship we possess all the blessings of God, yet we still at times do not see ourselves as worthy of His blessings that belong to every child of God.

The Curses of Deuteronomy 28

Deuteronomy 28: 15-45 AMP - The Curse

But if you will not obey the voice of the Lord your God, being watchful to do all His commandments and His statutes which I command you this day, then all these curses shall come upon you and overtake you. Cursed shall you be in the city and cursed shall you be in the field. Cursed shall be your basket and your kneading trough. Cursed shall be the fruit of your body, of your land, of the increase of your cattle and the young of your sheep. Cursed shall you be when you come in and cursed shall you be when you go out. The Lord shall send you curses, confusion, and rebuke in every enterprise to which you set your hand, until you are destroyed, perishing quickly because of the evil of your doings by which you have forsaken Me. The Lord will make the pestilence cling to you until He has consumed you from the land into which you go to possess. The Lord will smite you with consumption (diseases that cause the body to waste away like pulmonary tuberculosis), with fever and inflammation, fiery heat, sword and drought, blasting (diseases that cause the body to wither away and shrivel, it means to bring to ruin or destroy), mildew (all diseases of bacteria, fungus); they shall pursue you until you perish. The heavens over your head shall be brass and the earth under you shall be iron. The Lord shall make the rain of your land powdered soil and dust; from the heavens it shall come down upon you until you are destroyed. The Lord shall cause you to be struck down before your enemies, you shall go out one way against them and flee seven ways before them, and you shall be tossed to and fro and be a terror among all the kingdoms of the earth. And your dead body shall be food for all the birds of the air and the beasts of the earth, and there shall be no one to frighten them away. The Lord will smite you with the boils of Egypt and the tumors, the scurvy, and the itch from which you cannot be healed. The Lord will smite you with madness, and blindness and dismay of mind and heart. And you shall grope at noonday as the blind grope in darkness. And you shall not prosper in your ways; and you shall be only oppressed and robbed continually and there shall be no one to save you. You shall betroth a wife, but another man shall lie with her; you shall build a house but not live in it; you shall plant a vineyard, but not gather its grapes. Your ox shall be slain before your eyes, but you shall not eat of it; your donkey shall be violently taken away before your face and not be restored to you; your sheep shall be given to your enemies and you shall have no one to help you. Your sons and daughters shall be given to another people, and your eyes shall look and fail with longing for them all the day and there shall be no power in your hands to prevent it. And nations which you have not known shall eat up the fruit of your land and of all your labors, and you shall be only oppressed and crushed continually. So that you shall be driven mad by the sights which your eyes shall see. The Lord will smite you on the knees and on the legs with a sore boil that cannot be healed, from the sole of your foot to the top of your head. The Lord shall bring you and your King whom you have set over you to a nation which neither you nor your fathers have known, and there you shall be forced to serve other gods, of wood and stone. And you shall become an amazement, a proverb, and a byword among all the peoples to which the Lord will lead you. You shall carry much seed out into the field and shall gather little in, for the locust shall consume it. You shall plant vineyards and dress them but shall neither drink of the wine nor gather the grapes for the worm shall eat them. You shall have olive trees throughout all your territory, but you shall not anoint yourselves with the oil, for your olive trees shall drop their fruit. You shall beget sons and daughters, but shall not enjoy them, for they shall go into captivity. All your trees and the fruit of your ground shall the locusts possess. The transient stranger among you shall mount up higher and higher above you, and you shall come down lower and lower. He shall lend to you, but you shall not lend to him. He shall be the head and you shall be the tail. All these curses shall come upon you and shall pursue you and overtake you till you are destroyed, because you do not obey the voice of the Lord your God, to keep His commandments and His statutes which He commanded you.

All that the curses stated in the previous passage is what can come against us when we are separated from God or under the curse of the Law. Notice the effects of the curse are physical, spiritual and emotional. Most people have never taken the time to understand that these curses are what happens when we are separated from God. Even though we are not separated from God when we believe in Jesus, the devil tries to apply these curses to children of God. This happens because we do not understand that Jesus became a curse for us. We end up allowing the results of these curses to take ground in our lives.

Galatians 3:13,14 - NASB

Christ redeemed us from the curse of the Law, having become a curse for us - for it is written, cursed is everyone who is hung on a tree. In order that in Christ Jesus the blessing of Abraham might come to the gentiles so that we might receive the promise of the Spirit through faith.

All that we just read in Deuteronomy on the curse no longer applies to us. Jesus took that upon Himself for us. It says here that Jesus became a curse so that the blessings given to Abraham would now be ours through faith in Christ. So many times without realizing it, we allow the curses of Deuteronomy to function in our lives even though Jesus became a curse so we could have the blessing.

It would be like your parents dying and you were left a one million dollar inheritance. You then decided not to take the full blessing of the million dollars, but take $750,000 instead. No one would do that when it comes to money, so why would we want to allow the curses to take ground in our lives and not receive the fullness of the blessing that belongs to us. The Bible is like a legal document. It is binding and true, and it still applies to our lives today. The devil at times still tries to rob, steal, and destroy what belongs to us as a believer, so we need to enforce what belongs to us, and that includes the blessings of Deuteronomy 28, not the curses.

2nd Corinthians 5:21 - NASB

He made Him who knew no sin to be sin on our behalf, that we might become the righteousness of God in Him.

As the Lamb of God, the sin bearer, He was cut off from the presence of God, because, if you remember, to be cursed is to be separated from God. On the cross Jesus entered into the experience of being forsaken by the Father on our behalf. As in the Bible He said on the cross, "Father, Father why have you forsaken Me"? God turned His back on His Son so He would never have to turn His

The Keys to Inner Healing and Deliverance

back on us. Jesus was cut off from the Father and became
that curse.

The Blessings of Deuteronomy 28

Jesus became a curse and sin, and we are now the
righteousness of God because of Him. On the cross Jesus
took away the curses of the Law and only left the
blessings. He became that curse and took our place. Now
these are the blessings of Abraham that are now ours
through Christ Jesus.

Deuteronomy 28:2-14 - The Blessings - AMP

And all these blessings shall come upon you and overtake
you if you heed the voice of the Lord your God. Blessed
shall you be in the city and blessed shall you be in the field.
Blessed shall be the fruit of your body and the fruit of your
ground and the fruit of your beasts, the increase of your
cattle and the young of your flock. Blessed shall be your
basket and your kneading trough. Blessed shall you be
when you come in and blessed shall you be when you go
out. The Lord shall cause your enemies who rise up
against you to be defeated before your face; they shall
come out against you one way and flee before you seven
ways. The Lord shall command the blessing upon you in
your storehouse and in all that you undertake. And He will
bless you in the land which the Lord your God gives you.
The Lord will establish you as a people holy to Himself, as

He has sworn to you, if you keep the commandments of the Lord your God and walk in His ways. And all people of the earth shall see that you are called by the name (and in the presence of) the Lord, and they shall be afraid of you. And the Lord shall make you have a surplus of prosperity, through the fruit of your body, of your livestock, and of your ground, in the land which the Lord swore to your fathers to give you. The Lord shall open to you His good treasury, the heavens, to give the rain of your land in its season and to bless all the work of your hands; and you shall lend to many nations, but you shall not borrow. And the Lord shall make you the head, and not the tail, and you shall be above only and you shall not be beneath, if you heed the commandments of the Lord your God which I command you this day and are watchful to do them.

God's promise is to bring the blessings of being the righteousness of God to all who believe in the message of the gospel of Jesus Christ. That blessing and all that is in it now belongs to us. Jesus became a curse that we would receive the blessing of Abraham through Jesus Christ. So, is the enemy still trying to work those curses in your life, or is the blessing truly flowing to you? We have authority over the curse because Jesus became that curse for us. We no longer have to accept any of that curse in our lives. We can break the hold that it has on our life because it is already broken and conquered through the cross. It is finished, but we just have to realize it and apply it to our lives.

Prayer

The Lord has had me pray this prayer several times in church and in youth groups and the result was amazing as to how much even the youth testified that they felt releasing off of them.   The Lord has given us the authority to break every part of the curse that we may have inadvertently given room to in our lives. The Lord's heart truly is to release the storehouses and treasury of His blessings onto His Church.

Lord in Jesus name it says in Your Word that Jesus became a curse for us so that we would receive the blessing given to Abraham. So Lord in every place of my life, my finances, my job, my family, my health, and my body, that the enemy has tried to reinforce this curse, Lord I cover it in the blood of Jesus. Nullify, break, and loose it off of me and my family by the blood of the Lamb and the sword of the spirit in Jesus name. It is cut, severed, and broken by the blood of the Lamb and the sword of the Spirit in Jesus name from every area of my life. Thank you Lord that you became a curse so that I could receive those blessings in my life, not by anything I could ever do, but by what You did on the cross for me. Lord from this day forward I bind out the curses of Deuteronomy 28 and release the blessings into my life and into my family's life, in Jesus name. Lord let your storehouses of blessings flow from heaven to fill every part of our lives in Jesus name.

This blessing is not the name it and claim it theology, it is the blessing of God released upon our lives. A while ago a man came and sat down beside me at church and asked me to bless him, I was surprised and my first reaction was, Lord I am just a person, only you can bless. Then the Lord said to me, "no, pray the blessing of Deuteronomy 28 upon his life", for Deuteronomy 28 was the blessing that the Lord desired to have released upon him. It is always more powerful when you pray out scripture. As you are releasing the Word of God in prayer, it goes forward and accomplishes its purposes in our life, or in other's lives.   It is always wise to get into the habit of praying out scripture in your prayers for one another as much as possible. This is one scripture that we need to release and pray more often into the lives of our loved ones and the lives of our fellow brothers and sisters in Christ. Study the words of these passages in the Key Word Study Bible, or in the Hebrew. For when you do, you will find out how much the words mentioned in the Hebrew describe the diseases that mankind seems to fight to this day.

The Keys to Inner Healing and Deliverance

CHAPTER 13

MINISTERING IN THE AREA OF JUDGMENTS

The Bible is full of spiritual laws; for example the law of sowing and reaping, and the law of forgiveness. The spiritual realm is ordered by these spiritual laws, and one is the spiritual law of judgements, in how we judge, we will be judged. What brings confusion to the body of Christ is what we are called to judge. If the enemy keeps us judging the body, or individuals, then we end up bringing judgements against God's Church and people. It is important to know how or what to judge. Remember it says in the Bible in the Word of God, we do not fight against flesh and blood, or people, but the spirits behind what they do. Therefore we are not to judge people, but the spiritual workings behind their actions or words.

What We Are Called To Judge

1 John 4:1 - AMP

Beloved do not put faith in every spirit, but prove (test) the spirits to discover whether they proceed from God; for many false prophets have gone forth into the world.

As previously mentioned we are called to judge the spirits behind the person or action, but not the person themselves. We are to test the spirits and to discern if what happened is of God or of the devil; that is what we are to judge. There is a difference between trying the spirits and putting the individual on trial. Only God knows the motive of the heart behind what a person does. We cannot make any claim to know that, therefore we are not in a position to judge, only God can.

Matthew 7:15-20 - AMP

Beware of false prophets, who come to you dressed as sheep but inside they are devouring wolves. You will fully recognize them by their fruits. Do people pick grapes from thorns, or figs from thistles? Even so, every healthy (sound) tree bears good fruit (worthy of admiration), but the sickly (decaying, worthless) tree bears bad (worthless) fruit. A good (healthy) tree cannot bear bad (worthless) fruit, nor can a bad (diseased) tree bear excellent fruit (worthy of admiration). Every tree that does not bear good fruit is cut down and cast into the fire. Therefore you will fully know them by their fruits.

Another way to test the spirit moving behind an event or individual is the fruit of the spirit.

Galatians 5: 22-23 - NASB

But the fruit of the Spirit is love, joy, peace, patience, kindness, goodness, faithfulness, gentleness, self-control; against such things there is no law.

Is the fruit being produced and released through an individual the fruit of the spirit? Or is it the fruit of the flesh that the enemy uses? You will know them fully by their fruit if it is of God or not. For the fruit being produced will line up with the Word of God. Judge the fruit, but not the person. Otherwise we can judge the personalities more in individuals than the fruit itself. Jesus came into the world to save the world not condemn it. We were already condemned to a life separated from God, but now we are no longer separated because of what Jesus did on the cross. It has nothing to do with what we have done or not done, so none of us are in a position to judge an individual. Only the one that died for our sins is worthy of that call. So we are to test and judge the spirits behind people's actions, so that we can help them, pray for them, and bring restoration back to their life and ministry. Would we not want others to do exactly that for us as well?

Most of the time we judge what we do not understand, or we bring judgement on others because it makes us feel better about ourselves. If you come across something that you do not understand, or do not know if it is of God or not, then simply pray and ask the Lord if it is of Him. Simply ask God, "is this of You Lord, or is this of the enemy, or of the flesh, in Jesus name". The Lord will answer you and give you understanding about the person or the situation. In areas of judgement, or in any area of inner healing and deliverance, I asked the Lord many times in ministry to shine His light into the darkness to expose where the enemy is moving and how in any given situation so I can understand how to pray. Ask for God's wisdom, revelation, and understanding in the area you desire to learn about. He will give you that understanding, as it says in the Bible in His Word in Mathew 7:7, "ask and it shall be given you; seek, and you shall find; knock and it shall be opened to you". It is far better to receive revelation and wisdom than to judge what we do not understand. We really do tend to judge people and circumstances with only having a limited amount of information or knowledge. Only God knows all about every person or event, so only He is in the position to have all the information to form a judgement. So why not ask God for that understanding since He knows all, so we can judge the spirit behind it and not the person.

Matthew 7:1,2 Sermon on the Mount - AMP

Do not judge and criticize and condemn others, so that you may not be judged and criticized and condemned yourselves. For just as you judge and criticize and condemn others, you will be judged and criticized and condemned, and in accordance with the measure you (use to) deal out to others, it will be dealt out again to you.

This is so important for us to understand in ministry and in teaching. This is a spiritual law, for if we judge and criticize, or condemn others, we too will receive the same judgement. Also not only will this happen to us, but by the measure or degree in which we judge others, that will be the very same measure by which we will be judged. We really need to pause and think about this. How many times have we judged someone and the reason why they are in the predicament that they are in, and then it seems in no time we are in a similar type of situation? How different is our outlook when we are the ones in that predicament. We may think it is so unfair when it is happening to us, but the other person must have done something wrong to receive this type of mishap. See how critical and judgmental that really is. We need to realize the standard to which we hold others, is the same standard that we will also be held to.

The Church overall has been too critical in the lives of too many people, thus shutting them down. People end up walking in fear, condemnation, and in feelings of unworthiness of God's love, because of the areas they struggle in. We need to understand that only God is the righteous judge and jury, for only He can see the motive and intent of the heart. We are making a judgement based on incomplete information or appearances only. So if we cannot see everything, or know everything, then why do we think we are equipped to judge? We need to understand that we make judgements from our wounds, fears and misunderstandings. We make judgements many times based on the traumas of our past that we have walked through in our own lives. When we see similar things as adults happening before us, we then make similar judgements on those around us now. This means we are transferring judgements onto others due to past events and wounds. God understands our limitations, and that is why He asks that we leave all judgements to Him. However, He will give us the understanding of why someone is doing what they are doing so we can pray for them.

Matthew 7:3-5 - AMP

Why do you stare from without at the very small particle that is in your brother's eye but do not become aware of and consider the beam or timber that is in your own eye? You hypocrite, first get the beam of timber out of your own eye, and then you will see clearly to take the tiny particle out of your brother's eye.

We tend to look at everyone else's imperfections and faults and not at our own. It really is making a hypocritical self-righteous judgement against another person. I know that sounds harsh, but that is exactly how the Lord gave it to me. How can we really take something out of someone else's eye when we have something in our own?

Matthew 7:5 - NASB

You hypocrite, first take the log out of your own eye, and then you will see clearly to take the speck out of your brother's eye.

Have you ever wondered why Jesus used the eye and not another part of the body in this scripture? When we judge others while we have our own short comings, we really cannot see clearly to judge other people. All that is working through and hampering our own lives will also hamper our ability to see clearly and judge justly. That is why it is so important to get our own lives in order, and receive the healing we need, so we can be used as the body of Christ to help bring healing and restoration to others. The Lord's wisdom is so amazingly clear and simple, for when we deal with our own short comings we then have the compassion to help others in theirs. We are no longer actually judging the person, but wanting to truly help set them free. It is truly not right to judge the sins of others when we are still functioning in our own. You will also find that you will have more compassion for others in seeing how their areas of oppression hamper their lives, after you have spent time with the Lord dealing with your own.

Romans 2:1 - NASB

Therefore you are without excuse, every man of you who passes judgment, for in that you judge another, you condemn yourself; for you who judge practice the same things.

Romans 2:1 - AMP

Therefore you have no excuse or defense or justification, o man, whoever you are who judges and condemns another. For in posing as judge and passing sentence on another, you condemn yourself, because you who judge are habitually practicing the very same things (that you censure and denounce). (But) we know that the judgement (adverse verdict, sentence) of God falls justly and in accordance with truth upon those who practice such things.

This is something we have all read, but do we really

understand the ramifications of this scripture? If we are being honest as we judge others in the area of weakness, sin, or deceit that they have fallen into, most of us have fallen into that very same thing at some point in life. If not yesterday, then possibly tomorrow, so if we are not careful according to this verse, the judgement and condemnation that we released upon another now becomes ours. For as we judge so will we be judged; it is a spiritual law. We really without understanding it, condemn ourselves because we will all make the same mistakes. For scripture says what has happened to each one of us is not uncommon to man. We all go through the same types of trials, temptations, and sins. I want God's mercy in my life, which is His concern for the misery and consequences that my sin has brought into my life. So if I want God's compassion and concern for my misery then should I not have it for others? How can I get His mercy if I am handing out condemnation and judgement? When we do this we end up receiving the ramifications of the judgements that we have made on others in our own lives. When ministering to yourself, or to the body of Christ, you will find individuals will receive incredible freedom from the judgements that were made against them, or the ones that came upon their own lives by judging others.

There is only one true judge.

John 5: 26-30 - NASB

For just as the Father has life in Himself, even so He gave to the Son also to have life in Himself; And He gave Him authority to execute judgement because He is the Son of man. Do not marvel at this; for an hour is coming, in which all who are in the tombs shall hear His voice, and shall come forth; those who did the good deeds to a resurrection of life, those who committed the evil deeds to a resurrection of judgement. I can do nothing on My own initiative. As I hear, I judge; and My judgement is just, because I do not seek My own will, but the will of Him who sent Me.

We are to let Jesus be full judge, jury and to release Him to pass His verdict or sentence. He is the only one that knows the entire truth, and is the only one righteous enough to judge another person. None of us are qualified, or pure in heart to do it.   Only His heart is pure and holy enough and He is the only One who knows the full truth. As I stated before, only He knows the motive and intent of the heart because we cannot see into a person's soul, only He can.

Romans 14:13 - AMP

Then let us no more criticize and blame and pass judgement on one another, but rather decide and endeavor never to put a stumbling block or an obstacle or a hindrance in the way of a brother.

Now we are getting into how this works in ministry, but we needed to understand the truth of judgement first to be able to apply it into ministry. When we judge another and start openly stating how we are judging them, this is a form of accusation or judgement. It is as if we are putting in their way a large obstacle that is impeding them in moving forward in their lives and in the spirit. God had me perform this demonstration in church. For every judgement that I made against a person, I put a chair in front of them. For five judgements, there were five big chairs, or obstacles in front of that person. This demonstrated that my judgements against this person resulted in five obstacles being put there. I am so busy judging them that I did not realize that my judgements have actually made it harder for that person to get free, and to come out from under the sin or burden. I have inadvertently added to it in such a big way (eg. the chairs) that how could they ever possibly get free. How can Jesus restore them if I keep adding chairs or stumbling blocks in front of them? It has far more adverse effect on people's lives then we think. Whether we realize it or not, we are helping the enemy to accomplish his work when we do this. He loves it when we judge others. Why do you think that the very thing he wants us to be the most critical of is the Church and our fellow brothers and sisters in Christ? Remember we judge the spirit behind the person or action, but not the person. God told me years ago so as not to get hurt or take things personally, that when people would say unkind things about me, that I was to separate the person from the behavior. I was to separate the spirit behind the behavior or words from the person. It has made a huge difference in my life and my ability to minister. I understand it is the enemy trying to work through a person's life in areas of pain, to hamper or hurt me. It has made it so much easier to see these acts or words as chairs that the enemy is trying to put in front of me to stop me from going forward. This is why we do not want to put those chairs, or stumbling blocks in front of others.

Romans 14:13 - NASB

Therefore let us not judge one another anymore, but rather determine this – not to put an obstacle or a stumbling block in a brother's way.

Here is the kicker, for every chair or judgement that you put in front of a person, you may as well put one in front of yourself, because that is just what happened in the spiritual because of the spiritual law of judgement. That one hits with impact doesn't it? Every time you judge, you are judged, and by the same measure or the size of the chair or judgement that you placed in front of a person, the identical one is placed in front of you. How many of us would stand up and say God judge me as I judge others? That is what really happens in the spiritual, and then is manifested in the natural. It should make us think twice before we open our mouths, and look at the consequences of those judgements on others, and upon our own lives. It was really a very humbling revelation that the Lord placed in my heart.

How To Minister Judgements

The spirit of judgement unfortunately has filtered into the Church. Without realizing it we have become more critical and judgmental. Being critical and judgmental does not mean that we do not take a stand for truth, or the Word of God. We do, but we need to do it with compassion and love. For too many people, it has seemed that the church has had a closed door rather than a welcoming one. People have told me that they feel judged and unable to be themselves in the church, thus unable to open up about all that they struggle with. That has got to change for us to be effective in bringing in the harvest.

When dealing with an individual that has been very judgmental and critical, the first thing to remember is that it comes from their wounds and insecurities. So most likely that person is judging from that place of pain. Also the things we judge the most in others are the places we struggle with the most in ourselves.

The Lord showed me that with most people, due to past wounds, there can be a wall of denial, concealment, pride and self-righteousness. This has to come down, otherwise it would make it hard to release all judgements that we/they have either handed out or received. The enemy builds these walls so that we will leave all those judgements in place, because he understands the power of them in our lives.

Prayer To Bring Down The Walls Concealing Judgements

Lord, in Jesus name, cover the wall of denial, concealment, pride, and self-righteousness in the blood of Jesus and Lord bring down that wall that keeps your healing and freedom out in the name of Jesus. By the blood of the Lamb and the sword of the Spirit and by the hand of God the wall comes down now in Jesus name. Lord all denial, concealment, pride, and self-righteousness leaves now in Jesus name and every part of the wall comes down by the blood of the Lamb and the sword of the Spirit in Jesus name.

Give the Lord time to bring that wall down and ask the Lord to give you or them the eyes to see, the ears to hear, and the heart to understand what He is doing. Bind up and loose any guilt, shame, and condemnation the enemy would try to bring on you or them because of this. This is about you, them and others getting free, it is not about guilt or pointing the finger.

Prayer of Repentance To Remove All Judgements

Before we can release the judgements made by others off of our own lives, we have to make sure to first repent of judgements that we have made against others. That needs to be removed first, for how can we ask the Lord to remove something from us that we have done to others ourselves. This is key in the breaking off all judgements made against our own lives.

Prayer

Lord, I ask for forgiveness for speaking out judgements in other people's lives, please forgive me. I did not understand I was putting obstacles in front of them and hindering them, please forgive me Lord. Now I ask in Jesus name that You apply the blood to every obstacle, to every judgement that I have put in someone's life. Lord by Your blood nullify the effect of it off of their life and remove it now in Jesus name. Lord let it no longer be a hindrance in the name of Jesus. Lord I now ask that you apply the blood of the Lamb to every stumbling block that was put in my path through judgements, either from what others have spoken against me, or the obstacles I have put on my own path from judging others. Lord by the blood of the Lamb and the sword of the Spirit remove every judgement off of my life in Jesus name. By the blood of Jesus nullify every effect the judgements have made on my life and remove it in Jesus name. Lord remove every obstacle and every judgement against my life that was put in place by the spiritual law of judgment in Jesus name.

In ministry people have told me they have seen those stumbling blocks just blow up, and then be removed by the hand of God that were on their path. The thing that surprises most people from youth to adults is the number of people that God brings before them that have placed judgements upon their lives. It really is an eye opener for all of us to the degree we judge, the same degree others judge us, and how much it effects our lives.

Give the Lord time to speak to you or the person you are ministering to. Ask God for His truth about how the judgements have affected you and the others you are praying for. I have found that through the gift of the word of knowledge many times there will be other oppressions of the enemy that will also have to be prayed for after the judgements are released. Some of the oppressions that I have called out in this type of ministry beside judgmental and critical are sarcasm, negativity and skepticism. He may give you others, so just listen to Him and follow His leading to make sure you release everything that needs to be released.

CHAPTER 14

RELEASING VOWS

Vows are very powerful things, which although we make with good intentions, the enemy instead uses them to bind us up. Most people do not even realize that they have made a vow never mind being bound by them. This is an area that also brings much healing and freedom into a persons' life.

What Are Vows?

A vow is a solemn promise to do something or to behave in a certain way. It is to swear something or to promise something with which you are bound to. In other words, you are bound to the vow or oath you make, as well as all the conditions of that vow. We can make vows to God, vows to people, vows to the church, and inner vows which we make to ourselves.

Matthew 5:33-37 AMP

Again, you have heard that it was said to the men of old, you shall not swear falsely, but you shall perform your oaths to the Lord (as a religious duty). But I tell you, do not bind yourselves by an oath at all; either by heaven, for it is the throne of God; Or by the earth, for it is the footstool of His feet; or by Jerusalem, for it is the city of the Great King. And do not swear by your head, for you are not able to make a single hair white or black. Let your yes be simply yes, and your no be simply no; anything more than that comes from the evil one.

Notice it says do not bind yourself to an oath or vow. When you make a vow or oath you bind yourself to the words and the promises of that vow. It really is as if you set a trap for yourself. It is like you are in the forest and you are the one that is setting all these traps all around you. Because of the vows you made, it is like there is no way out of that forest without stepping on one of those traps. Those traps represent the promises that we really have no ability to keep every day all the time. It is impossible for any of us to keep the vows we make one hundred percent of the time. Therefore it is inevitable that we will step in one of those traps and be caught. That is why the Bible says anything more than a yes or a no is of the devil. God totally understands our inability to keep those vows or oaths.

James 5:12 - NASB

Above all, my brethren do not swear, either by heaven or by earth or with any other oath. But let your yes be yes or your no, no; so that you may not fall under judgement.

It Is Impossible To Keep Vows All The Time

Ecclesiastes 5:2-6 - AMP

Be not rash with your mouth, and let not your heart be hasty to utter a word before God. For God is in heaven, and you are on earth; therefore let your words be few. For a dream comes with much business and painful effort, and a fool's voice with many words. When you vow a vow or make a pledge to God, do not put off paying it; for God has no pleasure in fools (those who witlessly mock Him) Pay what you vow. It is better that you should not vow than that you should vow and not pay. Do not allow your mouth to cause your body to sin, and do not say before the messenger (the priest) that it was an error or mistake. Why should God be (made) angry at your voice and destroy the work of your hands?

Notice it says do not let your mouth or words cause your body to sin. You see when you make a vow you are really making a promise before God to keep that vow. When we do not keep that vow the words of your mouth cause your body to sin due to not keeping the vow or oath you made. Too many people just let vows or oaths fly from their mouths without understanding the consequences of not keeping them. Notice it says let your yes be yes and your no be no "lest you fall into judgement". When we inadvertently break those vows we unknowingly bring judgement upon ourselves.

We are made of flesh and our flesh is weak, no matter how hard we try we are never able to keep all our vows all the time without fail. Vows are about making promises for the future. The problem with that is our future is never certain and so many variables can come up that will cause us to have to break that vow. Vows whether we understand it or not, are made before God and therefore they bring in heavenly accountability to keep them. For it says in the Bible in the Word of God, to not keep them is to bring judgement upon yourself. Let's say you make a vow to volunteer once a week down at a shelter for the poor, but all of a sudden you cannot get down there because your kid or mom gets sick and you have to look after them. You have now broken that vow. When we break vows, guilt and shame is always around the corner, because we were unable to keep our word. Your heart was to do it, but because of unforeseen circumstances you were not able to keep your vow. That is what happens every time. God has taught me to change my words to "I will try to volunteer every week", understanding that something may come up from time to time that will prevent me from going.

Key Words Used In Vows

In vows we also use words I will never, and I will always. I will never be like my mom or dad. Sometimes we will use these words instead of words like I promise this or I promise that. Recognize the words "never" and "always" as words used in vows. They are words that are put forth stating that you will carry this out without fail. The vow of not being like my parents is one I have had to break off many people in inner healing and deliverance. That word never or always is your trap in the forest, because you are the son or daughter of that person and it is impossible to not be like them in some way. Many people because of being wounded by their parents will vow to never be like them. The problem is first of all, not all traits of our parents are bad, and some of them are good. We do not want to get rid of the good traits. Since you are their child, some of their traits will pass on to you, so now you have just set another trap for yourself that you will not be able to avoid. It is impossible to not be like your parents in some way, so this vow that so many make is impossible to keep, and the words in this type of vow will cause us to sin against ourselves.

Vows in Clubs Or Organizations

Many people also make vows or promises to organizations or clubs when entering in or joining. Be careful of these and understand what you are promising to do or not do because if it is too hard to keep you most likely will not be able to. Then you are accountable and in trouble once again. Do not just jump into saying these types of vows and promises in organizations. Really look into what it is that you are promising, for you will be held accountable to keep each one of those promises. It is also important to understand the moral and spiritual ramifications of what it is that you are promising. Remember God tells us to let our yes be yes and our no be no, and anything greater than that is of the devil.

Also many vows of secrecy are asked of people in organizations. Vows of secrecy are vows of entrapment that the enemy uses to keep people bound. Anything that puts you in a place of being secret and not being able to share what you are doing has red flags all over it. These vows will have to be broken and renounced in ministry as well as any other kind of vow made to release you from the legality of keeping them. Think of a vow or covenant in marriage and how sacred it is before God, and how binding it is in the physical and spiritual. All vows are like that, we forget we are really making promises or covenants before God and that we are now bound to the vow we made. We do not see the small print on that contract that binds us to the words we say. God made a covenant, promise, or vow with Abraham to give him and his descendants the Promised Land, from Egypt to the great river Euphrates. This was His covenant or vow to Abraham. God made this covenant because He is able to keep absolutely everything He promises. The Bible is a book of those very promises. We however, are not able to keep every promise being of flesh and a sinful nature.

How To Pray To Break Vows

In the case of a vow that you have made to promise to not be like someone, or to never do this or to always do that, it is very easy to break those vows before God. You will have to ask for forgiveness first understanding that God does not want us to make vows to start with. We need to now recognize our yes is yes, and our no is no. God wants to break you free from being bound to those words or stepping into the traps those words have established. For

He understands it is impossible for you to always be able to keep those vows. If the vow you made is one that you made to God, to others, or an inner vow to yourself. Pray as follows.

First ask the Lord to give you the eyes to see, the ears to hear, and the heart to understand where you have made vows in the past. Do this after you have bound every spirit according to Ephesians 6:12, released the anointing of God and the gifts of the Holy Spirit.

Prayer

Lord please forgive me for making this vow. I am so sorry, I did not understand that I was binding myself to those words. Lord I ask now that you cover that vow in the blood of Jesus and nullify and break it by the blood of the Lamb and the Sword of the Spirit, in Jesus name. Nullify it and release me from that vow now in Jesus name. Lord by the blood of the Lamb break every power of that vow off of every area of my life it has affected in Jesus name. Help me from this point forward to let my yes be yes and my no be no.

If the vows you have made are vows the enemy has used and have occult or witchcraft ties then not only do you need to repent for those vows but you need to renounce them before God. All vows of secrecy or vows that have occult ties will all have to be renounced before God.

Prayer

Lord please forgive me for making this vow or covenant. I am so sorry I did not understand that I was binding myself to those words, please forgive me in Jesus name. Lord I renounce in Jesus name any promise or vow to any organization or group I made in the past in Jesus name. Lord I put that vow under the blood of Jesus and nullify and break that vow off of my life by the blood of the Lamb and the sword of the Spirit. Lord I choose you as my Lord and Savior and I choose to follow your Word and the commandments of your Word in Jesus name. Lord by the blood of Jesus I break every power of that vow off of my life in Jesus name.

If you were sworn to secrecy in any organization, you will then have to also have a spirit of secrecy released off of you. The Lord may also give you through the word of knowledge other spirits that may have come in through that vow that also will have to be released off of you or a person's life. Just pray for example for that spirit of secrecy to be released from that person's life, mind, and heart in Jesus name. If it is an organization that the family has been involved in for generations then it will have to be cut to the third and fourth generation on the mother's and father's side as well, which was taught in a previous chapter.

The Lord knows your heart and your desire to do everything that you say you will do before the Lord. You do not need to jeopardize yourself by making vows or oaths that you cannot keep.

CHAPTER 15
SEVERING SOUL TIES

What Is A Soul Tie?

A soul tie ties or knits together two souls in the spirit realm. The bible does not call it tying two souls together but rather knitting together two souls, which even gives a greater picture of what a soul tie really is.

Colossians 2:2 - NASB

That their hearts may be encouraged having been knit together in love.

1 Chronicles 12:17 - KJV

David went out to meet them and said to them, if you have come peaceably unto me to help me, mine heart shall be knit unto you.

Think of the word knit. A soul tie is when your soul is knit together with another soul. So think of knitting or crocheting, when you knit something together as in two different colors of wool, once they are knitted together you no longer see each individual thread.   They have now become blended together making something completely different, a new pattern of sorts. Think of marriage ceremonies and why they do visual acts that represent the coming together of their hearts and souls like the blending of sand, or the lighting of two individual candles into one. These acts symbolize what is really happening when a soul tie is formed in marriage, but as we see above with David a soul tie can also be shared between two people other than just in marriage.

Ways Soul Ties Can Be Formed

The first way is a Godly way through marriage.

Ephesians 5:31 - KJV

For this cause shall a man leave his father and mother, and shall be joined unto his wife, and they two shall be one flesh.

The soul tie of marriage was created by God so that it would be an unbreakable bond, knitting two people together. This soul tie cannot be broken by man as it is in the spiritual realm in the soul of a man and a woman. Because God created man and woman, and the bond between them, the spiritual union of heart and soul, this tie can only be broken by the power of God.

Mark 10:7-9 - AMP

For this reason a man shall leave (behind) his father and his mother and be joined to his wife and cleave closely to her permanently. And the two shall become one flesh, so that they are no longer two but one flesh.

It shows that when a soul tie happens it really is when people are joined in the soul, and heart. It is as if they can move as one flesh. This is not just talking about sexual relations but the connection in the soul and heart of two individuals. It really is giving a part of who you are to another.

Another way soul ties can be established is through sexual

relationships outside of marriage. Where marriage establishes a Godly soul tie, sexual relationships outside of marriage establishes ungodly soul ties. This is why God commanded no sex before marriage. He understood the ramifications of having an ungodly soul tie, and the pain it can bring. For in sexual relationships even when people have intercourse in a casual way, it still results in one person giving a part of themselves to another. This is why when people in relationships break up, they still feel this connection that makes it hard to move on. They still feel drawn back to an individual even when the relationship may have been a toxic one. This is a result of that soul tie.

1 Corinthians 6:16 - KJV

What? Know ye not that which is joined to an harlot is one body? For two saith He shall be one flesh.

Through sexual relationships a piece of your soul is given to the other person, and a part of them is given to you. Remember, your soul is your heart, mind, will and emotions, all of what is given when we are involved in a sexual or deep relationship with someone. That is what it means to become one flesh. Those parts of one another are knit together. This can be very destructive especially in that today so many people have had so many sexual partners before marriage. Think about it, in each case where we have slept with someone we knit a part of our soul with the other, becoming one flesh, thus establishing a soul tie. God understood the pain that this can cause in His children. So many people that I minister to have soul ties with past relationships, which still causes so much pain in their lives to this day. It is as if they want to get away from that person but cannot. They know it is an unhealthy relationship and has hurt them in the past, but there is a draw to that person they cannot explain. That is because the soul tie is still in place. It keeps us connected to that individual even when we have tried to end the relationship with them. Some can even feel the draw to a person years after ending the relationship with them. This existing soul tie makes it so hard to go on and have a healthy and intimate relationship with another person until it is broken. Existing soul ties make it difficult to bond to a deep level in a new relationship while they are still in place.

Another way a soul tie can be established is through close relationships or friendships. You have soul ties with your children, with best friends, and special people in your life.

1 Samuel 18:1 - KJV

And it came to pass when he had made an end of speaking unto Saul, that the soul of Jonathan was knit with the soul of David and Jonathan loved him as his own soul.

This describes a soul tie in deep friendship. You genuinely care about the person, their heart and soul as you do your own when that soul tie is in place. I have always found that these soul ties are gifts from God and so special. You will feel a special deep love for that person even on a level you will not find with others. Those soul ties bring blessings into your life. Many Christians have had soul ties with spiritual mothers, fathers, and mentors that have been so instrumental in imparting to them spiritually. However, when these relationships either with friends, mentors, and leaders fall apart, these are often the relationships that leave the deepest wounds. They leave such a deep wound that seems to never really heal because of the soul tie that is still in place. There is still a spiritual soul tie to the person even though the person may no longer be in their lives. These types of soul ties will need to be cut. There also will be healing that will need to be released to the person as well.

As I stated before many times in abusive or bad relationships a person may leave and try to start new, but they keep feeling this pull back to that person even when they know it is toxic. At times people will find themselves going back to the person when they do not even want to be there. It seems they cannot help themselves; this is because of that soul tie. The soul ties, until broken, can keep the pain and anguish alive in a person's heart. This keeps a part of them from moving forward and receiving a complete healing. They end up continually reliving the pain over and over. In the case of deep Christian mentoring relationships where soul ties have been established, many have been hurt and wounded deeply and have had a hard time moving forward spiritually. They will find it hard to trust future pastors or even God because of those soul ties, and the wounds that came from those relationships. Severing all these soul ties can cause an instant release from those relationships that seem to have been over for a long period of time, but a part of them has never been able to move forward, for the pain still lingered. It is amazing how much healing enters into an individual's life when the soul ties are cut and the pain is removed by God.

For anyone who has had any soul ties with anyone practicing any form of witchcraft, those soul ties can act as cables through which ex-partners or close friends can send witchcraft. When those soul ties are cut the ability of ex-partners or friends to send anything through those soul ties ends due to the fact that the soul tie is now cut and severed. This is essential in doing ministry for yourself or others. It is imperative to have those ties cut in individuals that have had close relations with anyone in this area. Otherwise you will continually seem to battle spiritual oppressions or curses over and over due to this soul tie.

How To Break Soul Ties

Since soul ties are in the spiritual realm, only Jesus can break them. First of all you have to break all soul ties from any sexual relationships that you had before you were married. Then ask the Lord to show you any other deep relationships that are now over that carried a lot of pain where a soul tie was established. Some may be friends, mentors, and even Christian pastors or leaders.

Nevertheless, there was a deep connection of the soul that for some reason or another has now ended.

If there were deep relationships with a person whether in a relationship of marriage, mentoring, or best friends who were a part of your life for a longer period of time, you will have to first minister forgiveness before going into severing the soul tie. The person must first release forgiveness to that person for the Lord to completely sever that soul tie, and to bring a deeper and more complete healing. After that has been done, you will have to minister to them to allow the Lord to release all the pain and emotions that came through that relationship. You can then cut the soul tie. Make sure you give the Lord enough time to remove all spiritual oppressions that came through that relationship.

Prayer

Lord I understand that in this relationship we both have lost something and were both hurt. So Lord I forgive them and release them to you. In the name of Jesus Lord cut and sever the soul tie that I had with (name) by the blood of the Lamb and the sword of the Spirit, in Jesus name. Lord cut and sever it and place the blood where it was severed, for it never to be joined again, in Jesus name. Lord I ask you to release all sadness, sorrow, grief, and loss that this relationship caused in Jesus name. (The Lord may give you other emotions to release, just call them out as

God gives them.)

When ministering to past sexual relationships where there is no longer any relationship and really no pain left, but a soul tie was established, pray as follows.

Lord please forgive me for having sex outside of marriage and not understanding the ramifications of it. Lord I ask now in Jesus name you cut all soul ties between myself and (name) in Jesus name. By the blood of the Lamb and the sword of the Spirit, cut and sever the soul tie completely, and place the blood there so it will never be joined again, in the name of Jesus. Lord I ask you to remove all pain, sorrow, and grief that this relationship caused me.

Let the Lord show you any other emotion, or oppression that the Lord needs to release from your heart. Give Him a moment to show you what that is. For example, if the Lord shows you abandonment, then ask the Lord to remove all abandonment, in Jesus name. Do the same for each emotion the Lord shows you. Then ask Him to fill you with His love.

Soul ties are very powerful, and a person will feel incredible relief and closure in their lives in areas they never have before. You may find when ministering in the area of soul ties to yourself or others, you will have to go through several people with whom you or they have had soul ties. Follow the prayers above for each person that you or others have had soul ties with. Some relationships may require more extensive healing than others, as there may have been more emotional wounds through certain relationships. Either way, you will find an incredible relief through this kind of ministry. That pull to past relationships will release and you will receive closure and healing for your heart.

CHAPTER 16

PRIDE, ENTITLEMENT, AND FALSE HUMILITY

No one knows the power of pride to tear lives down better than the devil, for it was pride and a desire to exalt himself over God that got him tossed out of heaven. It is the same pride today that he uses to bring man down and to rob him of much.

Pride

Proverbs 16:18 - NASB

Pride goes before destruction and a haughty spirit before stumbling.

Pride leads to destruction and ruin. It changes our perspective from one of thinking of and serving others, to thinking of only self and what we deserve and want. Jesus was a servant above all, always serving everyone around Him. He was not self-serving, but about wanting to serve those He came to save. We think pride is so easy to detect in our lives but it is much harder than we think. Pride hides in the shadows of certain areas of our lives. However it is not necessarily in every area. God took me on a journey in my own life in this area to show me how hard it is to detect pride and even how much harder it is for the heart to give it up. The heart of God is to flush pride out of every person's life, because the enemy uses it to topple churches, ministries, men, and women.

But he gives us more grace, that is why scripture says God opposes the proud but gives grace to the humble.

Proverbs 16:5 - NASB

Everyone who is proud in heart is an abomination to the Lord.

Notice God opposes and detests the proud. Those are very strong words, but God understands the power of pride to bring down lives. Lucifer was the most beautiful angel in heaven, but his desire to elevate himself as God cost him everything. Pride separates us from God in areas of our lives, and it grows like a weed affecting and spreading over even more areas in our life in time. The word hubris also means pride, with the desire to be higher than God. This word certainly describes the heart of Lucifer at that time, but it also describes what pride can do to people when taken to an extreme.

It says in the Bible in Romans 12:3 " to not think of yourself more higher than you ought". Sometimes pride causes us to do exactly that in areas of our lives. God calls us to sober judgement which is very different. Also notice that pride goes straight to the heart, it does not just dwell in the mind, but it takes root in our hearts, making it much harder to detect and release.

God started me on a journey over a two week period, weeding pride and entitlement out of my life that I did not even know I had. The questions He posed to me would expose where I had let pride in. The first thing he told me was that I had passed the dreams that I had for my own life. As a result, I was now doing things for Jesus I had never dreamt that I would do and pride had gotten in. Jesus told me I had now taken on new dreams for my life since I had passed the ones I originally set. However, I had not surrendered these new dreams to God as I did with my previous dreams. I had not released them over to Jesus to allow Him to work them out the way He desired to. He told me I had to go back to being a servant not a leader. The Holy Spirit explained to me that Jesus never saw Himself as a leader, but as a servant of all. You see pride comes in when we see ourselves as superior in any way. The new dreams I had in Him, without me knowing it, caused me to see myself differently, no longer as a simple servant of God. God showed me that He wanted me to choose between being a leader or a servant before going forward. It was such a humbling and revelatory moment for me, as my head was willing to choose servanthood quickly, but it was like my heart would not follow. I was so surprised by this, to be honest, for I had always wanted to simply serve God. I thought about it for a moment, then I prayed and ask God to release pride from my heart. Once again I was taken aback. It was like there was a sticky gooey substance stuck to the pride that as I tried to get my heart to give it away, it just kept coming back. It really surprised me how hard it was for the heart to release pride to God. God wanted me to truly understand how hard it is to detect and release it personally.

God then spoke to me and said you need to serve, and have a servant's heart again in all things. He then stated, if the only way you serve Me is by teaching, equipping, mentoring, and praying for My people, even in small groups in back rooms, that you will serve Me in that place and be happy and content in it. Wow, well that was not what my mind was envisioning. I realized at that moment my heart was following the imagination of my mind in what I thought things would look like. This decision was not as easy as I thought it would be by any means. He then told me if I was to spend my time pouring out what I know to train people, and that if everyone I trained, taught, and mentored became much greater in the things of the Spirit than me then I had to be okay with that, and understand that is what it means to truly serve. You can kind of understand my shock to all of this, but also understanding in a deep way, it was such a moment of truth and Godly wisdom. The Kingdom of God is so different from that of the world and man. God wanted me to understand that to truly lead, in any way, a person must humble themselves to be the servant of many. Jesus is the greatest example of being a servant to many. Pride hinders us from doing exactly that. God truly humbled me in so many ways over that two week period, removing any pride that I had let in.

Jesus walks before us in all things. He is our guard, protector, and He clears our path from all that would obstruct us. He gives wisdom, knowledge and understanding for what is ahead. Pride however, puts us in front of Jesus standing ahead of Him, taking control. How smart is it for us to go in front of Jesus? In pride, it is as if we are saying we know more than He does. It is so important to continually go before Him and re-evaluate your dreams, where you are in Him, and to give all of your desires to God so He can work them out. When we do this we will give no place for pride and boastfulness. Is that not what the word says to do; to not give the enemy any place in our lives? We need to release expectation of what we think we are going to do and be, and choose that servants heart that pride tries to keep out.

Daniel 5:20 - NASB

But when his heart was lifted up and his spirit became so proud that he behaved arrogantly he was deposed from his royal throne, and his glory was taken away from him.

Daniel 5:20 - AMP

But when his heart became arrogant and hardened with pride, he was deposed from his royal throne and stripped of his glory.

Notice that at first this king became arrogant. That is the first step in becoming prideful; we become arrogant and boastful first. It is something we can learn to recognize with the help of the Holy Spirit. Notice the next thing that happens is that pride comes in and hardens our heart. The hardening of the heart makes it harder to hear or follow God in that area of our life. It also makes it harder to see the pride that we now have in our lives. That King was deposed due to the pride that had now hardened his heart. Deposed means to be removed from office suddenly and forcefully, overthrown, toppled, or to be displaced. All this happened because pride came into his life, this is what pride does.

Think of Pharaoh, and how he too thought of himself as a type of God, full of pride. This pride in the end cost him his son, his power, and so much in his kingdom. His people suffered so much due to his pride, with the ultimate destruction of his entire army. The most powerful army in all the land was toppled, overthrown and destroyed, because of pride. The cost of pride can be great.

This is exactly what happened to Lucifer in heaven. Lucifer wanting to be praised and worshiped like God caused him to be overthrown forcefully and displaced out of heaven. This is the power of pride working in any life. None of us are immune to it. It is a very powerful tool that the enemy uses, as he more than anyone else understands the destruction and cost it brings.

Flattering Words

The enemy can use the flattering words of others to do his work when we start going over and over those words, allowing them to puff us up. Boastfulness comes right before pride, and pride right before the fall.

Proverbs 26:28 - NASB

A lying tongue hates those it crushes, and a flattering mouth works ruin.

Proverbs 29:5 - NASB

A man who flatters his neighbor is spreading a net for his steps.

The enemy will play the flattering words that someone else wanted to bless us with, over and over to slowly puff us up so that we become boastful. The enemy's desire is for it to grow into pride. It is a slow process which is why at times it is so hard to see where pride is, unless we allow the Holy Spirit to show us. The enemy can use flattering words to deceive our hearts, which in turn changes our perspective, causing us to make decisions and do things based on those flattering words.

I asked the Lord how to stop the enemy from using flattering words to cause us to fall into this trap, as we still need to receive the thanks and compliments from others. Those words are their way of blessing us, and we would rob them of that blessing to not thank them and receive their kind words. The Lord instructed me to always know in our hearts that it is the Holy Spirit working through us that does all things and without Jesus and the Holy Spirit showing up nothing would happen. It is the Holy Spirit working His gifts through our lives that causes things to take place. So when we honor God and give Him the glory in what has happened through our lives, it keeps boastfulness and pride at bay. So receive those words with thankfulness, but if you hear them going over and over in your mind, ask the Lord to remove boastfulness, for all things come through Jesus. Start thanking Him for all He is doing through your life, professing that every move of His Spirit comes from and through Him.   Those words will stop going over and over again in your mind. You will once again have your heart and mind focused on Jesus and not on flattering words.

Humility

We are called to a place of humility. It is the complete opposite of what pride is. Humility sees a need for a savior, for forgiveness, grace, mercy, and a need for God's strength and help in all things. Humility does not see all of this though at the expense of our own self-worth or identity.

Humility is self-giving, and self-sacrificing for the sake of others. Humility encourages, serves, and cares for others. It treats everyone with respect and concern regardless of position and status. People with humility have a servant's heart, ready to serve, without seeking any personal gain. Humility makes it easy to receive feedback, correction, and training. It allows a balanced view of self, understanding personal strengths and weaknesses, and the role that each of us will play in God's Kingdom. It is truly having a Kingdom perspective instead of a self-perspective. When we go from thinking of others and God's Kingdom to thinking of ourselves, we have then started that journey from humility to pride. Jesus was the greatest example of all by living a life full of humility. He served all humanity to the point of laying down His life, while never dismissing His self-worth or the worth of others. Jesus truly demonstrated perfect humility.

Jesus intrinsically values everyone. Humility can celebrate another person's gifts and talents without comparison. Jesus did not compare Himself to anyone, but saw each person's uniqueness, gifts, and talents. He celebrated each person's value and importance on this earth to God. He touched, spoke and taught thousands, but then He washed the feet of His disciples and reached out to the out casts of society. He never saw anyone less than Himself. Pride sees ourselves as superior in some way to others; humility is thankful for what we have, and sees no one greater than another, just different. Jesus never acted like He was above or better than anyone.

Humility and a servant's heart caused Him to serve all, even though many fell away from the faith. Only a small number followed Jesus' instructions to the Upper Room, yet He still served every person, even the ones He knew would reject Him. This is how humility is, the complete opposite to pride.

False Humility

Colossians 2:18 - NIV

Do not let anyone who delights in false humility and the worship of angels disqualify you. Such a person also goes into great detail about what they have seen, they are puffed up with idle notions by their unspiritual mind.

False humility looks like humility, sounds like humility, but it is really insecurity. In false humility you are not able to receive compliments. When someone compliments you, false humility hears the compliment, but because of responding from a place of insecurity, one then dismisses the compliments that were given. A false humility mindset can often sound comparative, comparing oneself to others around them. It sees others as greater than themselves, but not from a place of servanthood, but from a place of low self-worth or low self-esteem.

False humility belittles oneself due to feeling inferior. When we have false humility we can often be people pleasers. False humility causes us to be timid and insecure, afraid to take the initiative and speak up. It can cause us to be dependent on what others think and say about us. It can also cause us to be scared of correction and feedback due to low self-esteem.

Humility never puts one's self down, compares or sees others or themselves as less, that is false humility. Humility knows and understands ones identity and worth in God, but focuses on the gratefulness to the Lord for what they have been given. In humility, one desires to serve what they have been given to those around them. False humility sees or feels they have very little to offer those around them. Jesus was by far the greatest example of humility. He came to serve all mankind to the point of death.

Entitlement

Another area many of us struggle with is entitlement, not really recognizing it or how it affects us. You could call it the brother to pride, for it tears down people, families, and ministries, just as pride does.

Matthew 20:1-16 - NASB

For the kingdom of heaven is like a landowner who went out early in the morning to hire laborers for his vineyard. And when he had agreed with the laborers for a denarius for the day, he sent them into his vineyard. And he went out about the third hour and saw others standing idle in the market place; and to those he said, you too go into the vineyard and whatever is right I will give you. And so they went. Again he went out about the sixth and the ninth hour, and did the same thing. And about the eleventh hour he went out, and found others standing and he said to them, why have you been standing idle all day long? They said to him because no one hired us. He said to them, You too go into the vineyard. And when evening had come, the owner of the vineyard said to his foreman, call the laborers and pay them their wages, beginning with the last group to the first. And when those hired about the eleventh hour came, each one received a denarius. And when those hired first came they thought that they would receive more; and they also received each one a denarius. And when they received it, they grumbled at the landowner, saying, these last men have worked only one hour, and you have made them equal to us who have borne the burden and the scorching heat of the day. But he answered and said to one of them, friend I am doing you no wrong; did you not agree with me for a denarius? Take what is yours and go your way, but I wish to give to this last man the same as to you. Is it not lawful for me to do what I wish with what is my own? Or is your eye envious because I am generous? Thus the last shall be first, and the first last.

Notice that the ones who worked the longest felt entitled to have more than those who worked less. It is amazing how we all can feel entitled to so much without really knowing it.

The Lord decided to take me on another journey to show me how entitlement creeps into our lives. I was about to speak at a fall conference that we put on every October when just before the conference there was a new anointing in which I started to function in. It was one of healing for the physical body more than just the mind and heart. It was really amazing how the anointing moved and how detailed the prayers were when in this anointing. The results of the prayers were immediate. It was the night before I was to speak at the conference that the Lord decided to show me I had entitlement. It was in the early hours of the morning when the Lord spoke to me and revealed I had entitlement. He said because I had prayed and stood in places for Him over a long period of time that I had felt entitled that God would use me in the conference to pour out His anointing. How wrong I was. He told me that I was entitled to nothing, that God chooses who He wants to use and when. None of us are entitled to anything, for even the gifts of the spirit belong to God and are used by the Holy Spirit. He also told me that He is a sovereign God and that He is able to do all things on His own, but chooses to bless us by giving us the blessing of partnering with Him. I had no idea that I had this, but what God was saying was truly eye opening to say the least. It made me start to go over my life and see if there was anywhere else I felt entitled, even in the area of serving God.

I then repented for having entitlement, and asked God to release it. He showed me that sometimes when we serve God for a while and have pressed through many things for Him, that entitlement can come in because of the hard place we have had to stand. It was a humbling moment for me, but what was more humbling was God did not use that anointing at the conference. It truly saddened my heart. My next thought was what if the women lost out because of me? What happened if they could have received more, but because of my feelings of being entitled they did not? God let me sit on that thought for a period of time, about a week. It was to let me understand the magnitude of what pride and entitlement can not only rob us of, but how it can also rob those around us. God in His mercy though gave me a blessing. I received a note from someone who went to the conference telling me how she and all of her friends had received so much healing and were so grateful for the move of God. That was such a relief, and I thanked Jesus. Then the Lord spoke to me and said do not think that what you are struggling with will cause the people I brought to not receive all that I wanted to give them. He reminded me that He is a sovereign God, and did not need me for Him to pour out to His people. I was so thankful and relieved that no one was robbed of the blessing. What I realized is that the one who lost out was me. It was a lesson that was so profound in my heart. I am sharing all this with you because I know so many of us have either been in this type of situation or could be in the future, if not in ministry, in places of work, or in family situations.

Just like the parable said, the Lord is lawful to give what He will when He chooses, to whom He chooses. We are all so blessed to have the Lord share moments of Himself and His work with us. Stay in a place of humility, and know that all God does through our lives, all that He uses us for, are truly gifts from Him.

Prayers For Pride and All That Can Come In With Pride

Lord I bind every spirit according to Ephesians 6:12 and I release your anointing and gifts of the Spirit in Jesus name. Lord I ask you to give me the eyes to see, ears to hear, and heart to understand where pride is in my life in Jesus name. Shine your light of truth and expose where and when it came in Lord. (Give the Holy Spirit time to show you where the pride is.) Jesus I repent, and am sorry for allowing pride into my life. Lord I ask that you release all pride from my heart and life now, in Jesus name, by the blood of the lamb and the sword of the spirit release all pride from my heart, in Jesus name. Lord release all pride, and boastfulness, in Jesus name. Lord release pride from every area of my life that affected my ability to hear you Lord, and move greater in your gifts of the Spirit, in Jesus name.

The following may also have come in with pride so you may need to pray these off as well.

Lord in Jesus name release all stubbornness, boastfulness, and arrogance, in Jesus name. Lord release it all by the blood of the lamb and the sword of the spirit, cut sever and break off all stubbornness, boastfulness and arrogance, in Jesus name. Lord also release any and all jealousy, usurption, control, and superiority, by the blood of the lamb and the sword of the spirit, in Jesus name. Cut, sever, and break it off of my heart, mind, and body, in Jesus name. Lord also release all of being unteachable off of my heart and mind by the blood of the lamb and the sword of the spirit in Jesus name.

Prayers For Entitlement And All That Can Come in With It

Lord Jesus I ask for forgiveness for all entitlement that I have let into my life, please forgive me. Lord I ask you to cut, sever, break, and loose by the blood of the lamb and the sword of the spirit all entitlement from my mind, heart, body, and life in Jesus name. Release it all Lord, break it off of every part of my life in Jesus name. Lord I also ask you to break off all jealousy and envy that has also come in, in Jesus name, break it off by the blood of the lamb. Lord also release off of my heart, mind, and life, any feelings that I have been cheated out of something that I have felt entitled to, in Jesus name. For Lord I am entitled to nothing, all that I have is a gift from You. Life itself is a precious gift from you Lord. Thank you for all you have given me, for your mercy and grace that you shed upon my life in Jesus name.

Prayers for False Humility And All That Can Come In With It

Lord I ask you to release all false humility that I have in any area of my life, in Jesus name. Lord cut, sever, and break it by the blood of the lamb and the sword of the spirit, off of my mind, heart, body, and off of every part of my life it has affected, in Jesus name. Lord I also ask you to release all

insecurity, and low self-esteem off of my mind and heart,
in Jesus name by the blood of the lamb and the sword of
the spirit, in Jesus name, release it all Lord. Lord release
all timidity and fear of speaking out, off of every area of
my life, by the blood of the lamb and the sword of the
spirit, in Jesus name, release it all Lord. Lord I also ask you
to release by the blood of the lamb all people pleasing, off
of every area of my life, where false humility has caused
me to desire to please people and has put me in bondage,
in Jesus name. Lord give me the eyes to see, ears to hear,
and the heart to understand my true worth in You in Jesus
name. Help me to see myself through your eyes and heart
from this point on.

These prayers are basic prayers to release pride,
entitlement, and false humility from your life, as well as
areas of oppression that can come in with it. Always know
the Lord may give you other things that came in through
pride, false humility, and entitlement that you may need
to also pray and release. God may also bring up situations
that pride or entitlement came in through so ask for
forgiveness and allow the Lord to release pride and
entitlement from those individual situations as those
would have been the roots that pride entered through.
Ask the Lord if there are any other roots where pride,
entitlement, or false humility came in. That way there are
no root systems left where pride can be built back up
again in your life. Simply follow the basic prayers above to
release whatever it is that God revealed to you.
Remember these prayers are only guides to help you

understand what to pray, but as you become more comfortable following the Lord you will find your prayers will grow as you follow the Holy Spirit more rather than these individual prayers I have listed. Each individual will also have their own style of praying that is comfortable for them. As long as the basics of the prayer are in there how you exactly pray does not affect the way the Lord will answer your prayers. He hears the cries of your heart, and honors you coming to Him to receive healing and understanding. It brings joy to the Lord's heart when we come desiring to go deep into our lives and into Him to find freedom.

.

CHAPTER 17

UNWORTHINESS AND INADEQUACY

So much of our lives are affected by how we see ourselves. Feelings of unworthiness and inadequacy can truly cause us to settle for less, make bad decisions, and react in ways that sell ourselves short, therefore diminishing our own worth. The choices we make in our lives are relational to how we see our own worth.

We all have feelings of unworthiness and inadequacy due to past failures and heartaches. A lot of the time we have pain and fear about our future, and it really is not about the future, but more about our past.

One of the people God showed me as an example of this in the Bible, which at first glance I would never have seen as feeling unworthy or inadequate, was Moses. In the Bible in Exodus 2:11-15, Moses kills an Egyptian who was beating upon a Hebrew man. He then decides to bury him in the sand to hide what he had done. Pharaoh discovers this, resulting in his desire to kill Moses which causes Moses to take refuge in the land of Midian. Much of our unworthiness can come from circumstances in our past. Moses most likely would have felt so bad about killing the Egyptian, yet so consumed with anger at the same time. So when God called him to his mission he most certainly would have felt unworthy due to the mistakes he had made in his past.

Do not let your past hold you back. We do not need to let it hinder us from doing great things for God. What we have done or what has happened in the past can be serious, but there is a great God that loves us and is eagerly waiting to save, heal, deliver, and restore us through what Jesus did on the cross. Even though Moses killed a man, God had forgiven him, and was calling him to one of the most incredible missions ever: to set His people free.

God's heart is for not one of us to feel unworthy or inadequate in anyway. God will provide for us what we need in our present situations. He is always reaching out His healing hands so we can move into the fullness of our destiny in Him. He does not let our past dictate our future in Him, so why do we? God is more than able to do anything with your life. He has already forgiven you of your past mistakes, so do not bring those mistakes from the past into your future.

Exodus 3:2-8 - AMP

The Angel of the Lord appeared to him in a flame of fire out of the midst of a bush; and he looked and behold, the bush burned with fire, yet was not consumed. And Moses said, I will now turn aside and see this great sight, why the bush is not burned. And when the Lord saw that he turned aside to see, God called to him out of the midst of the bush and said, Moses, Moses! And he said, Here am I. God said, do not come near; put your shoes off your feet, for the place on which you stand is holy ground. Also He said, I am the God of your father, the God of Abraham, the God of Isaac, and the God of Jacob. And Moses hid his face, for he was afraid to look at God. And the Lord said, I have surely seen the affliction of My people who are in

Egypt, and have heard their cry because of their taskmasters and oppressors; for I know their sorrows and sufferings and trials. I have come down to deliver them out of the hand and power of the Egyptians and to bring them up out of that land to a land good and large, a land flowing with milk and honey.

Moses sees a bush burning and as he approaches he realizes the bush is not being consumed by the fire. He then hears the voice of God speaking to him. What a miraculous sight. God then gives him definite instructions of what He desires to give His people, freedom. You would think hearing the voice of God, knowing it was His voice, and seeing the bush consumed by fire would be enough for him to believe all of what God was speaking to him, but it wasn't.

Unworthiness and inadequacy causes us to doubt what God is saying to us regarding ourselves or our situation. God's word to Moses was instructional and personal. God spoke to him and told him, I know what my people are going through. I have come down to save My people, and I am going to send you to set them free. Moses however still doubted God and his own ability to do any of what God was calling him to do. When we feel unworthy or inadequate we focus more on what we are feeling rather than what God is saying about us, our situation or Himself. How many of us have known God has spoken to us, by placing something on our hearts concerning what He desires to do or give us in our lives? Yet in our own unworthiness we doubt Him, even when we knew it was God who was speaking.

Relationships we choose, things we settle for in life, and the decisions we make are a mirror or reflection of how we see our own worth. The enemy understands this more than you know. He understands that if we feel inadequate, or unworthy, then our actions and choices in life will never line up with the fullness of what God has for us, or what He can do through our lives.

The mirror of how God sees us when it is held up would be a very different reflection than the reflection in which we tend to see ourselves. When I have prayed this before in ministry it is amazing to see the difference between the two reflections that people see. What they felt was the true reflection was a counterfeit and false to how God truly sees them.

Instead of learning what God says about our worth and identity in the Bible, we tend to listen to our past or people instead. We need to learn to trust what the Word and God says about our worth. Why do we doubt the very God that created the universe, instead listening to the voice of self or the enemy?

When God was saying in Exodus in the Bible "I will bring you up out of your afflictions" He was talking about His power and ability to change their circumstances. There is nothing too hard for God, and what He does is not dependent upon our worth or how we see ourselves, but on what God wants to bless us with. You see God was trying to tell Moses through the burning bush, I see you as worthy, I see you as My son, able to do all things through My power. I am choosing you to do this, because I love you. Why do we impose our abilities and worth onto what God can do, and expect Him to only move within our abilities and worth, not His own?

Exodus 3:11 - AMP

And Moses said to God, who am I that I should go to Pharaoh and bring the Israelites out of Egypt.

Moses was responding to God through his own feelings of worthlessness and inadequacy. Moses felt he lacked the qualities needed for the job. He was looking into the reflection that he erected which said he did not have the ability, qualities, or worth for the job. How many of us say and feel this way before God? Do we not think God is more than able to furnish all we need to do whatever it is He wants to bless us with? God was more than able to do anything through Moses, and God is able to do more than anything through us.

Exodus 4:1 - AMP

And Moses answered, but behold, they will not believe me or listen to and obey my voice, for they will say, the Lord has not appeared to you.

Exodus 4:10 - AMP

And Moses said to the Lord, I am not eloquent or a man of words, neither before nor since You have spoken to Your servant; for I am slow of speech and have a heavy and awkward tongue.

Moses was full of doubts and unworthiness, consistently not focusing on God but on all his shortcomings. Do we not think God is more than able to overcome all of our shortcomings? Do we not think He can change, gift, and bless us with all we need? How many times has God said I will do this in your life, and this will happen, and we know it is God speaking, but we still did not believe Him. Our own feelings of unworthiness and inadequacy get in the way.

God was raising up a mighty leader, but that leader still saw an incapable, inadequate, and unworthy vessel. God saw and chose exactly who He wanted. He is looking at each of you, and choosing you, knowing you are exactly who He wants for the job. God was saying I want you Moses, and Moses was saying you do not want me. That is what unworthiness does; it disqualifies us from what God wants to do through and in our lives. It causes us to truly think God can find better. Moses kept coming up with excuse after excuse as to why not him. I smiled at this because when I was younger I was jokingly known as the woman with many excuses. I could come up with an excuse for pretty much anything. Well that no longer works with God. God no longer would allow me to discredit myself. He wanted me to stop looking in the mirror of unworthiness and inadequacy, so He turned me to the true reflection, His reflection of who I am in Him. It truly was the complete opposite to the reflection I had seen for so many years. Low self-esteem, unworthiness, inadequacy, and feelings of being incapable cause us to not accept what plans the Lord has for us. It causes us to make decisions that we would have never made otherwise. It causes us to lose out on tremendous blessings from God because we feel unable in any way to achieve or receive what God wants to give.

Verse 4: 12,13 - NASB

Now then go, and I, even I, will be with your mouth, and teach you what you are to say. But he said, Please Lord, now send the message by whomever Thou wilt.

In other words, God please send someone else, whomever you choose. What would happen if God really listened to us when we said God send someone else? We need to thank the Lord that He does not listen to us! That the Lord keeps seeking after us, desiring to use and bless us, even when we cannot see our own worth or value. God spoke something to my heart that was truly profound. He said, "Do not call anything unworthy or inadequate that I have saved and called worthy through what I did on the cross." This one sentence sums it all up. God sees each one of us through His Son, each one capable of so much more than we ever dreamed.

Prayers for Unworthiness and Inadequacy

These are the prayers for unworthiness and inadequacy.

Lord in Jesus name bind everything according to Ephesians 6:12, release your gifts of the Spirit and Your anointing to me, in Jesus name. Lord reveal to me the reflection of how I have seen myself and my worth in Jesus name. (Let Him show you visually or reveal it to you by thought or impression on your heart.)

Lord, in Jesus name, I ask you to remove all unworthiness and inadequacy by the blood of the Lamb and the sword of the Spirit, to the third and fourth generation on my mother and fathers' side in Jesus name. Lord, release it off of my mind, heart and body, in Jesus name. Jesus remove it off of every part of my life, off my relationships, job, and my destiny in You. Lord, in Jesus name, also remove all low self-esteem, incapability, and insecurity to the third and fourth generation on my mother and father's sides, in Jesus name. Cut, sever, and release it Lord, by the blood of the Lamb and the sword of the Spirit from my mind, heart, body and life in Jesus name.

Lord I ask You to now show me the mirror that reflects my true worth in you Jesus. Give me the eyes to see, the ears to hear, and the heart to understand my true worth in You, in Jesus name. Lord release from my mind and heart all false images of my worth that the enemy or self placed within, in Jesus name. Lord give me the ability to walk away from the false habit patterns of unworthiness and inadequacy, in Jesus name. Thank you Lord that I am seen as worthy and loved by You, and that you have chosen me, and desire to walk with me, now and always.

Make sure you take time to let the Lord speak to your heart on this issue. He will speak to everyone differently, but He will impress upon your heart all that He desires you to understand and know. He will also deposit in your heart, His heart towards you, and how much He truly loves you, and how He sees you as His son or daughter.

CHAPTER 18
DENIAL

Denial is another weapon the enemy uses in areas of our lives to prevent the healing process, so that we can be set free in areas of oppression. It also impedes the sanctification process. We are to be perfected, becoming more Christ like, which is what happens in the healing and sanctification process. Salvation means to be continually saved in all areas of our lives, continually healed, continually delivered, continually restored, which happens through our healing and sanctification process. Denial acts like a wall that prevents the healing process of God from penetrating the deep wounds in our lives.

Hebrews 4:12 - NASB

For the Word of God is living and active and sharper than any two edged sword and, piercing as far as the division of soul and spirit, both of joints and marrow, and is able to judge the thoughts and intents of the heart.

Denial acts like a giant wall, impeding the ability of the Word of God to do its work in an individual's life. It also acts as a barrier to the sanctification and healing process. It blocks out the power of the Word and truth to go in to your heart and expose the works of the enemy in our lives. Thus preventing our healing and sanctification which then prevents us from walking in the freedom of Jesus.

The definition of denial in the Greek translation in the Key Word Study Bible is the refusal of something requested, a refusal to comply to God, or with His request. Denial is a refusal to accept a belief in something that the Holy Spirit or someone is trying to show you. It is an unconscious defense mechanism characterized by refusal to acknowledge painful realities, thoughts or feelings. Denial is a close relative to disobedience and holds hands with pride.

Denial stops us from achieving freedom or walking into the fullness of our destiny. Denial prevents the Word of God and the Holy Spirit from sanctifying us. All strongholds hidden behind the walls of denial will remain upright until denial is removed, as it acts as a barrier preventing access. We have to first admit that we have this particular problem in our lives, confessing to denial as the Holy Spirit reveals it to us allows it then to be removed. The healing process can then begin with all that was hidden behind those walls of denial.

Denial makes it hard for God to change all mindsets, false belief patterns, and habit patterns that have been put in place through traumas and painful events in our lives. Denial will say, I do not have any false belief systems or that problem in my life. I do not have that pain, I really am fine. I do not suffer from this oppression. That is why in twelve step programs the first step is to admit that you have a problem, because before that is done the healing process cannot begin. Denial hides the darkness of oppression in our lives. The enemy understands this, and the more he can keep hidden and away from the light of God, the more we will remain in our present state of bondage. This is the power of denial and why the enemy uses it.

Ephesians 4: 11-13 - NASB

And He gave some as apostles, some as prophets, and some evangelists and some pastors and teachers, for the equipping of the Saints for the work of services, to the building up of the body of Christ; until we all attain to the unity of the faith and of the knowledge of the Son of God to a mature man, to the measure of the stature which belongs to the fullness of Christ.

Denial stops us from coming into unity with the Spirit and into the full knowledge of Jesus Christ. It also hinders our ability to become mature in the things of God, thus attaining the whole measure of God. Denial says I am fine, nothing needs to be changed in me. Denial is basically saying whatever God and any spiritual mentors are saying regarding your life is wrong. As denial grows and greater levels of deceit enter in because of it, it makes it much harder for Holy Spirit to teach, guide and correct us. We end up resisting the help that the Holy Spirit wants to give us in areas of oppression where denial is.

Proverbs 12:1 - NASB

Whoever loves discipline loves knowledge, but he who hates reproof is stupid.

2 Timothy 3:16 - NASB

All scripture is inspired out by God and profitable for

The Keys to Inner Healing and Deliverance

teaching, for reproof, for correction, and for training in righteousness.

Denial prevents us from being taught and corrected by the Holy Spirit, thus stopping our spiritual growth. As previously mentioned, denial hates reproof and joins hands with pride. We need to let the Holy Spirit put His finger on the areas of our life that need work or healing. We need to allow Jesus to point out areas of disobedience or wherever we are hindered. When we ask God to expose any areas of denial, and allow Him to remove that denial, we will then be able to see what was hiding behind it thus growing in faith and becoming more like Him. Only then will we be able to truly be set free in the area that denial is concealing. When denial is removed, we will truly know the truth of our circumstances, the strongholds in our life, resulting in freedom. It is time to take down these walls of denial and let God truly heal you fully. Do not allow the enemy to say you are weak, or cause you shame or humiliation because you have denial. Understand that it is purely a tactic of the enemy to keep us bound. Let the Lord truly free you from the cage where denial has entrapped you.

Prayer for Denial

Lord, in Jesus name, I ask you to give me the eyes to see, the ears to hear, and the heart to understand the areas of my life where I may have denial, in Jesus name. Lord, I

198

bind everything that is trying to block me from seeing that denial, and I ask you to remove it out of the way, in Jesus name, that I may see it. Lord shine your light into the darkness and expose all denial, in Jesus name (Give the Lord a few minutes to show you areas where that denial is operating and what it is covering.)

Lord, in Jesus name, remove all denial now by the blood of the Lamb and the sword of the Spirit. All denial in my life now is being removed by the hand of God. Lord, every wall of denial comes down now by the blood of the Lamb and the sword of the Spirit and by the hand of the living God. Lord remove it all so that I may now see all that was concealed behind that denial, in Jesus name. Lord also all concealment and containment that hid that denial and what was behind it also leaves now by the blood of the Lamb and the sword of the Spirit, in Jesus name. Lord, any pride, disobedience, and doubt that may have come in with denial I ask that you remove it all now by the blood of the Lamb and the sword of the Spirit, in Jesus name. Lord remove it all from my mind, heart and from hearing the truth of what is happening in my life. Lord I give you full Lordship over this area in Jesus name.

Due to the fact that denial was covering hidden areas in your life that may need healing, the Lord will now direct you to what exactly needs to be prayed for now the wall of denial is gone. You can now go back to the other sections of the book if you are not sure how to pray for what he is showing you that is behind the denial. Allow the Lord to go in and heal the areas that denial was covering. If there is any shame or embarrassment that you are feeling because of what is hidden, just ask the Lord to remove it in Jesus name. He hears your prayers and answers them and it brings great joy to His heart that you come to Him in prayer and supplication. He will meet you there for you are His child and He loves you greatly.

CHAPTER 19

FEAR AND DREAD

The enemy more than anything else tries to keep us stationary, unable to move forward in God, and nothing accomplishes that more than fear. Fear keeps us stationary. It is like standing in a pair of cement boots unable to move. The phrase "Fear not" is written 103 times in the bible. Fear is spoken of so many times over and over, because the Lord knows how much it is used to keep us from walking into the fullness of God, or to have healing in areas of oppression.

The definition of fear in the Greek translation of the Key Word Study Bible is to be put in fear, alarm or fright, to flee, terror, astonishment, trembling, to cause to run away, object of fear or alarm, a state of being anxious, timid and timidity. All of which causes us to turn from the Lord and to see what we fear as bigger than God. Fear is actually the opposite of faith. For in fear we no longer see God as able to overcome. We see the fear as being larger and in control.

2nd Timothy 1:7 - KJV

For God has not given us the spirit of fear, but of power, and of love, and of a sound mind.

Notice he is first teaching the church that there is a spirit of fear with which the enemy wants us to be oppressed with. Fear is an emotion that we all deal with. That emotion is called being afraid. However, when fear takes on a level where it over takes an area of our life, oppressing us constantly, then it is usually a spirit of fear that is oppressing us.

To be in fear is to have unbelief or doubt in God and His ability. We doubt that God is big enough at that moment to overcome whatever it is we are facing, or having to go through. Fear can also come in through trauma and situations in our life that have deeply affected us. Fear's biggest job is to get us to doubt God, and to allow the enemy to take us captive in the area in which we are afraid.

When I was in grade one I had three bullies that were in grade seven tackle me one afternoon after school in a field that I used to walk through to get home. They proceeded to bury my head in the snow. They sat on my head for what felt like eternity. I actually saw things go black for a moment because I could not breathe. Then I heard a faint voice of an adult call out and say, "Get off of her". They immediately got off of me and ran away. I did not realize this at first, but ever since that event I became claustrophobic, totally fearful of enclosed places. I could not go through tunnels in playgrounds, or be anywhere where I could be trapped in an enclosed environment by someone. I did not realize where this came from until one day God revealed it to me and showed me the root of my fear. He went in and brought emotional and physical healing to me. He released all the fear that had held me captive. It was amazing how much fear had oppressed me in that area of my life, as I remember not being able to go into caves on our holidays or into any enclosed spaces.

Fear truly can be an incredible stronghold in your life.

Different Levels of Fear

Fear really does come in different levels. It is important to recognize the different levels of fear in our lives.

Timidity

One of the lowest forms of fear is timidity. Timidity causes us to shy away from anything that we feel may be too much for us. It causes us to withdraw and retreat, not extending ourselves out of our comfort zone.   Through timidity we will not walk into the fullness of God because of pulling back from new things in our life. Timidity brings feelings of inadequacy and shyness.   We become very reserved, unassuming, and not wanting to be the center of attention. So even though a person may be very talented, naturally or in the spirit, a timid person will want to remain in the background in a supportive role. They do not desire in any way to be in the forefront, or for any attention to be placed on them.   Many times when people are released of timidity they become more outgoing and more willing to try new things in life.

1 Chronicles 22: 13 - KJV

.....be strong and of good courage, dread not nor be dismayed.

Dread

Dread is another level of fear, which means to anticipate something with alarm, reluctance, and fearful or distasteful anticipation. To dread something is really a low stage of fear. When you dread something, you really do not want to do whatever it is you are dreading. You dwell on it to the point that the thought of doing it just seems overwhelming. You really are in fear; fear of not being able to accomplish a task or to walk through what is in front of you. You dread what you are to do, feeling inadequate and incapable. It plays over and over in your mind till it builds up into something insurmountable. You just want to avoid it at all costs. This is really a type of fear, a lie that has been planted telling you that you cannot accomplish something or overcome your circumstance. Dread tells you that doing this will bring no joy or peace to your life, and in fact, it will cause you more harm. The enemy wants us to believe this lie, which will cause us to dread something. Dread then becomes fear that leads to doubt in the ability of God to move in our life in this area. We then are locked by that fear, as we end up immobilized, stationary, and unable to move forward in this area. We are now fully oppressed by fear in a certain area of our life. We have now embraced the fear, causing us to choose to remain in our circumstances because of the power that fear now has over us.

Phobias

From timidity and dread you move into greater fears and anxieties that cause you to truly be trapped in the fear that is in your heart and mind. Phobias are the greatest degrees of fear, which cause us to be paralyzed in those areas. There are many different types of phobias that people can suffer from. If a person has any phobia, when doing ministry it is crucial to name the phobia and command it to leave, in Jesus name. Phobias can actually cause a person to adjust their entire life. That phobia has now taken total control over their life and has entrapped them in many ways.

Fear Controls and Brings Torment

Isaiah 41:10 - NASB

Do not fear, for I am with you; do not anxiously look about you, for I am your God, I will strengthen you, surely I will help you, surely I will uphold you with My righteous right hand.

The enemy does not care if he pushes you back as long as he keeps you from moving forward. Fear keeps us stuck but God is more than able to be what we need Him to be in every area of our life. In fear we tend to panic more and make rash decisions based on our emotions, instead of being directed by God. Fear will rule our actions and reactions if we allow it to, causing us to walk further from

God in areas in our life. This causes the stronghold to grow greater and more effective. When free, fear will not rule our decisions. Fear also causes us to blow things up out of proportion, making what is really a small situation into something enormous. We then see this mountain in front of us that seems insurmountable. It could have been conquered so easily if we had just let God in to release it. To continue to move forward in life in power and strength with God we need to remain the same in the storm as when there is no storm. Fear does not allow us to do that. Fear causes us to focus our attention on the storm and the lies and fears of the enemy, instead of the love and power of God.

1 John 4: 18-19 - KJV

There is no fear in love, but perfect love casts out fear; because fear has torment. He that fears is not made perfect in love. We love Him because He loved us first.

God's heart is that we have no fear, for He understands that fear torments our souls and robs us of peace and an abundant life. Torment means affliction, punishment, and harassment. This is not the heart of God for His children's lives. Fear brings torment and robs us of faith and love that the Lord desires to give each one of us. We receive opportunities and blessings from the Lord, but fear comes from the devil.

The torment that comes from fear causes much anxiety and depression. Now more than ever before, mankind is suffering from so much anxiety, depression and fear. It says in the Bible in the Word of God in 1 John 4:18-19, "perfect love casts out fear". Only God's love is perfect love. Perfect love is a complete love in that it never wavers or changes. His perfect love lacks in nothing, and is perfect till the end of time. Man's love is not a perfect love, but God's is, and that is why it is a love that can cast out all fear. This love gives us freedom from all fear and the anxiety that torments us and holds us back. The love of God is unconditional and ever flowing. It is a love that we need to understand as the Church of Christ, that when we allow it to flow through our lives freely it is amazingly powerful and transforming, releasing all fear in people's lives. When the perfect love of Jesus flows to others or ourselves, we truly will see people set free from fears that have held them captive for a long time. There is so much power in the love of God. It was through that love that God sent His Son to the cross. It is through that love that Jesus gave His life. In the Bible in John 15:13 it states, "Greater love has no one than this, that one should lay down his life for his friends". It is this love that sets us free.

Many Different Types of Fears

There are many types of fear, and through ministry I have discovered how much more powerful it is to name the actual fear than to just tell fear to leave. For example there is a fear of failure, a fear of not doing enough, a fear of not being enough, a fear of crowds, a fear of not getting things right, a fear of people not liking us, and the list goes on. I used to just ask fear to leave, but one day the Lord was teaching me about fear and He explained how different the fear of failure moved in a person's life compared to a fear of being in crowds. That is why to name the particular fear that the Lord gives you is far more powerful. It pinpoints the area of fear, how it affects our life, and really releases it more completely than if we do not name it. It also gives us or a person we are ministering to an understanding of the fear and how it moved in our life. God always wants to bring understanding and revelation to every area of our life when He ministers to us. As the Lord shows you each root of the fear, as with my phobia from bullying, we command that fear to leave from that root, in Jesus name. We then become free of that particular fear. Where there is fear, the enemy exerts his control in that area of our life, making it harder for the Lord to move. If God wants us to speak and teach about His Word to people, but we have a fear of crowds or a fear of public speaking, then it will be much harder for God to move in our lives and raise us up as a speaker. Those fears would now hinder us and God's ability to move and release us into our calling. When the different types of fears are removed, then God is able to come in and speak truth and truly free us from the captivity that the fear brought into our life.

When I was first walking with the Lord and learning to hear His voice, I got a message from God, or so I thought. I was wrong though, as it was not Him, but it was the enemy, trying to send me on a wild goose chase. I told those closest to me that God had told me I was pregnant and wanted to extend our family, but what I discovered in time was it was really the enemy trying to get me off of God's work. It sent me into a tailspin, especially emotionally, because there was a part of me wondering whether or not to have more kids and the enemy played right into that. I told people I had heard this but then I discovered it was not God. I felt ashamed, guilty, like I really did not hear from God at all. I just wanted to shut down and keep quiet. I immediately let in a spirit of fear of getting things wrong and not hearing God. It had a dramatic effect on my life, as I had even gone to the extent of getting an ultra sound to make sure I was not pregnant. I stopped trying to hear God for myself. I started relying on others around me because I was too afraid of getting it wrong again. I was listening to people that did not hear God any better than myself, but to me at that moment in fear, it seemed wiser. I was making decisions through that fear. It kept me silent and for six years I was no longer speaking out what God was giving me. The Lord kept talking but I was too afraid to speak it out to anyone. I was afraid I did not really hear from Him. It truly shut down a huge part of my walk and growth with God. In time, God showed me what I had done and He spoke something truly profound to me. His truth set me free. He said to me that if a toddler does not walk the first time they try, are you going to tell the toddler, oh well you could not walk the first time so I am going to give you a wheelchair and you can sit in that now instead of walking? I pondered that for two seconds and I thought that seems silly why I would do that. There was a pause and He said, "No sillier than just because you heard incorrectly one time and were deceived that you felt you needed to shut down and not speak out again". He was right but that was really what that fear had done to me. God went in and delivered me from all fear of not hearing God properly. The ironic part about this was the enemy knew exactly what God was calling me to do in ministry. The key to the type of ministry I do now is hearing and following the Lord and His directions. The enemy knew if he could silence me and put fear in this area it would stop me from fulfilling my calling and moving into this type of ministry to help others. I see it all now, but back then I was controlled by that fear. It is truly amazing how fear binds us up.

Psalm 34:4 - KJV

I sought the Lord, and He heard me and delivered me from all my fears.

We need to run to our fears, not away from them. God hears us and He says He will deliver us from all of them. We need to trust Him and know He is able to do this. Our fear traps us in a cage and prevents us from moving forward. Fear causes us, instead of focusing on God and what He is saying, to focus on the devil and what he is saying. Do not panic and look at your own strength or ability. Look to God and know that you are doing all things through His strength and His ability. No longer believe the lies of the enemy. Hear the words of the Lord, and know through His perfect love and the power of the cross, that He is more than able to deliver you from every fear. He took all your fears onto Himself on the cross. It is already a finished work. Allow Him to release off of you all that He already has victory over. Walk in the perfect love of God, instead of the fear of the enemy. All that Jesus did was motivated by love, and it is that love that truly sets you free of all fear.

Prayer for Dread

Lord I bind every spirit according to Ephesians 6:12, I ask you release your anointing and your gifts of the Spirit. Lord, in Jesus name, I ask you to show me where I may have dread in my life. Give me the eyes to see, the ears to hear, and the heart to understand. (Give the Lord a moment to show you where any dread may be). Lord in Jesus name I ask you to remove all dread by the blood of the Lamb and the sword of the spirit, release it off of my mind and heart, in Jesus name. Lord I ask where that dread was and that you replace it with your perfect love. For Lord I can and will do all things through Your strength and love, in Jesus name.

Prayer for Fear

Lord, I ask you to show me, in Jesus name, every root of fear that I have in my life. Lord give me the eyes to see, the ears to hear, and the heart to understand, in Jesus name. Lord, shine your light and truth into my life and expose all roots of fear, in Jesus name. (As before, give the Lord a moment to show you roots of fear, there may be more than one so you may need to do this prayer over a few times. He may reveal to you all your fears over a period of time due to the amount of fears that bind you.) Lord, give me a spirit of understanding and revelation of how this operated in my life, in Jesus name. (He may speak to you or just give you an understanding of how this fear worked in your life, and also what type of fear it is.) Lord, in Jesus name by the blood of the Lamb and the sword of the Spirit cut, sever, and break off all <u>fear of failure</u> in Jesus name. (Insert any fear God gives you into where I gave an example of the fear of failure.) Break it off of my mind, my heart, and my body, in Jesus name. (If you know it runs in your family, also pray the following to cut it in the generations, as fear can be generational) Lord cut and sever it to the third and fourth generation on my mother and father's side in Jesus name. Release all of the fear off of every part of my life in Jesus name. Lord, I ask you to fill me with your perfect love, as it says in the Bible, "perfect love casts out fear", so Lord release your perfect love into every area of my life where fear was, and fill every part of my mind and heart with your perfect love in Jesus name.

God may also give you other things to pray off that came in through the fear, for example, insecurities, timidity, and unworthiness. Simply command them to leave in the name of Jesus as well.

The Lord wants each of us to walk in the perfect love of God, not bound in the shackles of fear.

CHAPTER 20

HEALING IN UTERO

Utero inner healing means receiving inner healing and deliverance by actually allowing God to take you back to the time of being in the womb itself. You will find in inner healing and deliverance that at times people will receive much healing by going back to the womb itself.

Psalms 139: 13-16 - NASB

For You did form my inward part; You did knit me together in my mother's womb. I will give thanks to You, for I am fearfully and wonderfully made. Wonderful are Your works. And my soul knows it very well. My frame was not hidden from You. When I was made in secret and skillfully wrought in the depths of the earth, Your eyes have seen my unformed substance....

Isaiah 44:2 - NASB

Thus says the Lord who made you and formed you from the womb, who will help you. Do not fear....

Jeremiah 1:5 - NASB

Before I formed you in the womb I knew you. And before you were born I consecrated you; I have appointed you a prophet to the nations.

Notice not only did God know us in the womb, but He also knew us before He formed us in the womb. This means our souls, our heart mind will and emotions, was already formed and known by God before we were even placed in our mother's womb. This is truly incredible and amazing!

We were all placed in our mother's womb with a purpose, with the God of all nations knowing us and who we are. Remember your soul is who you are, and it says He knew us, and that word knew in the Hebrew language means not to just know someone, but to intimately know someone. He intimately knew each one of us even before we were in our mothers' womb.

That is the spiritual aspect of us in the womb. In the natural, the baby's mind starts recording while the baby is still in the womb. Remember your soul is your heart, mind, will, and emotions, which God formed and knew intimately before He placed you in our mother's womb. That is why doctors speak about the importance of the bond between a mother and a child, and how it is formed in the womb. In the natural, the soul, the heart of who you are, is recording early in a child in utero. That is why some inner healing and deliverance goes back to when a person is in the womb.

When my children were newborns, although they could not focus or see clearly, they recognized my voice as mom, when I was feeding them, or speaking to them. That is why doctors speak about the importance of playing music, talking, and reading to the unborn child. Children can also sense the touching and rubbing of the stomach by the mother's gentle touch. The child records the entire stimulus and is able to recognize it outside of the womb. For even at the time of being in the womb, everything is recorded in the subconscious or deep seated mind. The unborn child in utero records all that is happening around him or her.

The emotional and physical state and well-being of the mother also directly affects the baby. We understand through medical studies how the physical health of a mom affects the physical health of the unborn child. However, the emotional state of the mother also has direct ramifications on an unborn baby as well. For example, if a mom suffers from depression or anxiety, the baby is able to feel that emotion and records it. The bond between a mother and child is so strong in utero. Many times the Lord will take a person back to the womb to release all the depression, feelings of sadness, sorrow, and anxiety that they felt from the mother in the womb. The feelings they feel from the mother as a child in utero can cause the child to make false assumptions of not being loved or wanted, which can directly affect them throughout their life. I know this seems unlikely, but you would be surprised how many times incredible healing comes from the place of the womb. These can be emotions that are released through inner healing, or there can be spiritual oppressions attached that also need to be released through deliverance. Either way, it is an easy thing for the Lord to do, and His tenderness and love in this area always amazes me.

In a session I did a long time ago with a young woman, she was amazed that she was taken back to the womb. She found herself in utero where she heard, to her amazement, the sound of her mother's heartbeat in the womb. She stated it was so loud in her ear; it was as if she was back in the womb in that moment. It was so amazing to her. The Lord then revealed to her how as a baby in utero, she felt all the sadness and depression of her mom. This was also coupled with sorrow and feelings of despair. The Lord went into the womb with that little one and removed all of the depression and sadness and took every feeling that told her that she was not truly loved or wanted by her mother. The Lord showed her the truth of why her mom was in the state she was in, and that her mother's depression had nothing to do with her. The Lord spoke truth into her heart and brought total healing to that little baby in the womb. She immediately felt everything being released from deep within her. These healings happen far more often than you would think.

In surprise pregnancies the mom can often battle with whether or not they want a child, and then they struggle with the changes that may take place in their lives. The baby will also feel this emotion and record it. Many times the unborn child will feel unwanted, rejected, and unloved. As adults we can reason out why it would have been a struggle for the mother in surprise pregnancies. We can reason how it would have changed their life and the fears they would have had to process through. As an adult we could still reason and understand all of this while still knowing that we were loved. However, the baby in the womb has no defenses and feels all those emotions that the mother is going through, emotions of fear, and of confusion of even desiring whether to be pregnant or not. Babies really have no ability to process or reason this through. In fact a child up to the age of about six has no mental defense in the area of wounds of the heart or mind. For this reason younger children or the unborn still in the womb experience wounds or trauma that go much deeper than those children who are older. So the baby in the womb ends up feeling all those emotions of not being wanted, or that they are a burden. The Lord is able to go back into the womb and heal that little one, thus releasing the pain or condemnation from them as an adult, and how they currently see themselves. This is not to place guilt or condemnation on the mother in any way. It is merely to explain why some children have these issues later on in life.

If there was physical or emotional abuse to the mom during pregnancy the children, no matter the age now, will most likely need inner healing and deliverance in the womb for what they were feeling at the time. There will be issues of fear, rejection, abuse, and feelings of being unsafe that will also have to be released off of that baby in utero. The lies that the little one took in, absorbed, and later believed in the womb, as well as the false assumptions as to them not being loved, wanted or needed will also have to be released. Just like before, let the Lord, through the gifts of the Spirit, and word of knowledge, direct you to release all that the little one took in at that time. In this type of ministry for yourself, it is always advisable to have someone there with you, as it is too hard to hear what the Lord is saying to you and minister in this area at the same time. The person you are praying with will also be able to give you other emotions that need to be released that you may not have heard through the gift of knowledge.

When you have released everything as the Lord directs make sure you give the Lord time to speak to that baby in the womb. He will show them their true worth, value, and identity in Him. Jesus will explain how much they mean to Him and how much they are wanted and cherished. For many believe they were a mistake, which is the farthest thing from the truth. I felt I was a mistake because of my adoption. The Lord took me into the deepest place and showed me how he had a plan for my life and how I was born with a purpose. Jesus showed me that nothing about my life was a mistake. He showed me every detail was planned and orchestrated by Him. It truly made a huge impact and difference in my life. It changed how I saw myself, and helped me understand that my life meant something. My life was important to Jesus. He planned to use it just as He plans to use each one of your lives for something good. This type of ministry truly makes a profound change in a person's life and how they see themselves, I am a great example of just that. He really does give us beauty for ashes.

Another area that you will always find healing is just outside the womb or after birth especially in the area of adoption. As I stated earlier, I was adopted so I truly understand this. An adopted child will consistently have some level of rejection, abandonment, and feelings of not being loved, wanted or needed. They will also deal with fears in every one of those areas as well. In cases of adoption there will always be a level of inner healing and deliverance needed in the womb or just after birth. In the womb, the child will often feel the feelings of the mother's struggle to give up the baby at birth. There will be fears, insecurities, and rejection in the womb to deal with. The Lord released all of that from my life, and all the false assumptions that caused me to make bad choices from that place as I became an adult. The Lord went into that place in my heart and truly showed me the value of my life to Him, which brought total healing to my heart and soul.

In cases where you are dealing with a person that is a twin, you can also deal with certain issues in the womb and through the birthing process. Sometimes depending on how they were situated in the womb you will come across different issues of what one is feeling over the other. In some cases, when one twin is born first, the second one may experience feelings of being left behind and can feel separation anxiety in the womb from being left alone until the time of their birth. Also physically hard deliveries or tough pregnancies can cause fears and trauma to an unborn child that the Lord is also able to go in and bring release and healing to. As in all inner healing and deliverance, it is always so important to let the Lord dictate and lead, no matter what information you are getting. Always let Him direct you. Our job is just to follow His leading in the healing process, even when praying for ourselves. We may know where more pain is in our lives, but follow God's leading in the order He dictates. He knows the best way, and the best timing for all ministry.

I also received much healing connected to the time right after birth. It was only a few years ago that I had raised one of my spiritual daughters in the Lord and I knew it was time to release her and to let her soar in Jesus. Somehow though I could not do it, which was contrary to all I knew I was meant to do in the Lord. So I went to Jesus and asked Him why it was so hard for me to release her and asked Him where the root was. He took me to the crib in the hospital just after I was born. I saw myself all alone and the Lord spoke to me that I was alone for over a month in the hospital waiting to be taken to my adoptive parents. As a result I felt all alone and that no one wanted or needed me. The Lord started to release off of me in that crib all that I was feeling and showed me that I had a lack of touch, or of being held since I was alone for so long. I did not feel secure or safe. He released all of that from me in that place, but He told me that the biggest part was that I had such a fear of not being needed by someone. Jesus told me this was where the inability to release my spiritual daughter came from, and how this was holding me back from being able to release her into her calling. It truly was a fear that if I let her go I would no longer be needed. The Lord then went in to my heart and mind and released all of those fears, and brought total healing to that area. The next thing He showed me was profound and I will never forget it. He showed me how I was never alone in that crib and how He came and held me all the time. He showed me that I had angels all around me at all times, watching over me. Then He spoke these words to me that had such power and love in them, He told me He will always need me. It really was one of the most profound and healing moments that came into my life. Amazingly enough, literally one month later, my mom (adopted mom) gave me my legal adoption papers of when I was adopted. These papers showed that I was in the hospital for 32 days after I was born before I was taken to my mom and dad. Now that is God!! God even gave me proof of what I had received my healing for. Just know that in every area of your life that there is hurt or pain, the Lord already knows, and can bring total healing to you through His love for you. Even in the miraculous healing of the womb, God comes in and brings incredible healing that profoundly affects the person as an adult to this day.

CONCLUSION

The Keys To Inner Healing and Deliverance will provide you with foundational subject matter that most people seem to deal with when struggling with oppression. By developing a greater understanding of these principles, God may lead you into a greater depth of inner healing and deliverance in various situations that may occur. As God leads you into greater depths, the same principles as taught here will apply to each situation that the Lord brings to your attention. God's heart is to cover and honor the prayers of every believer when we truly seek God and His freedom in every area of our life. You will find as you become more proficient in your prayers that you will start to combine many of these sections into one prayer for yourself or others. God truly wants to reveal Himself in the area of healing of the heart, mind and body to the Body of Christ, so the Church may function from a place of freedom and victory, and not from a desert place of bondage and struggle.

DISCLAIMER

This book and its prayers are simply guidelines to give you instruction and information regarding inner healing and deliverance. As you learn to listen to the Holy Spirit and grow in your ability to hear Him and move in the Spirit, one will develop their own unique style of praying.

The contents of this book are to be solely used in the area of inner healing and deliverance and by no means are to replace psychiatric evaluation or medical support. Inner healing and deliverance ministry is entirely led by the leading and directing of the Holy Spirit, to heal the broken hearted and set the captives free in the body of Christ in mind, body, soul and spirit. No person should take on inner healing or deliverance that is beyond their capabilities in knowledge, wisdom, or understanding in this area of ministry. It is always best to have another person present when entering into any type of ministry.